OCCASIONAL PAPER 140

Government Reform in New Zealand

Graham C. Scott

INTERNATIONAL MONETARY FUND
Washington DC
October 1996

Cataloging-in-Publication Data

Scott, Graham C. (Graham Cecil), 1942-
Government reform in New Zealand/Graham C. Scott
—Washington, DC: International Monetary Fund, [1996]
p. cm. — (Occasional Paper, ISSN 0251-6365; 140)
ISBN 1-55775-540-X
1. Administrative agencies—New Zealand. 2. Organizational change—New Zealand. 3. Government productivity—New Zealand. 4. New Zealand—Politics and government—1972– I.Series: Occasional paper (International Monetary Fund) ; no.140.
JQ5829.O73 S36 1996

Price: US$15.00
(US$12.00 to full-time faculty members and
students at universities and colleges)

Please send orders to:
International Monetary Fund, Publication Services
700 19th Street, N.W., Washington, D.C. 20431, U.S.A.
Tel.: (202) 623-7430 Telefax: (202) 623-7201
Internet: publications@imf.org

recycled paper

2050 7066

Contents

Appendix

Charts Section

Figures Section

Appendix

The following symbols have been used throughout this paper:

. . . to indicate that data are not available;

— to indicate that the figure is zero or less than half the final digit shown, or that the item does not exist;

– between years or months (e.g., 1991–92 or January–June) to indicate the years or months covered, including the beginning and ending years or months;

/ between years (e.g., 1991/92) to indicate a crop or fiscal (financial) year.

"Billion" means a thousand million.

Minor discrepancies between constituent figures and totals are due to rounding.

Preface

The reforms to the systems of government management in New Zealand that are discussed in this report arose from an immense effort by some of New Zealand's leading politicians in recent times and from the commitments of senior civil servants who instituted a regime that ultimately affected the working environments of tens of thousands of civil servants throughout the country. Without their determined efforts to design and implement these changes, I would have no report to write. The leadership at the political level for these reforms came from Roger Douglas, David Caygill, Richard Prebble, Stan Rodger, and Geoffrey Palmer on the Labor side of the Parliament and from Ruth Richardson and Bill Birch on the National side.

In the central agencies, the key figures in the State Services Commission were Roderick Deane, Margaret Bazley, Don Hunn, and Doug Martin. The Auditor-General, Brian Tyler, while at arm's length, was a key supporter of the changes. In the Treasury, which I had the pleasure to head through most of the changes described here, the entire department put in an extraordinary effort over many years to make this happen. I currently manage my own consulting firm in New Zealand and I am also a Principal of Law and Economics Consulting Group Inc. of Emeryville, California.

Space allows me to acknowledge the contribution only of those senior managers who carried most of the responsibility for this effort. They are Howard Fancy, John Chetwin, Ian Ball, Andrew Weeks, Mark Byers, Peter Bushnell, David Smyth, Irene Taylor, Graeme Wheeler, Pat Duignan, and the current Secretary to the Treasury, Murray Horn. Individuals who undertook the technical design of the Public Finance Act in particular were Tony Dale and Peter Lorimer.

I am indebted to the following people for assisting me in the preparation of this report: Michael Palairet of the New Zealand Defence Force; June Pallot of the Department of the Auditor-General; William Maguire of Auckland University; Andrew Weeks of Financial Management Resources; Paul Blessington of KPMG Consulting Group in Canberra; Alex Matheson of the State Services Commission; and Doug Martin of Martin, Jenkins de Lore. At the Treasury, Roger Beckett, Elizabeth Ashton, Howard Fancy, Mark Byers, Richard Morris, and Ken Warren provided me with information.

For comments on the first draft, I am indebted to Alan Tait, Masakazu Sakaguchi, Barry Potter, and Chris Yandle of the International Monetary Fund (IMF), when I served as a Consultant at the Fiscal Affairs Department from April to June 1994; and to Malcolm Holmes of the World Bank. Ian Ball, of Victoria University of Wellington, provided particularly valuable comments on the second draft. For the preparation of the document itself, I am indebted to Mary Thomson of the IMF and to Carole Hoult in Wellington; and to Jacqueline Walters of the Fiscal Affairs Department (IMF) for correcting successive drafts of the document. Simon Willson and Martha Bonilla of the External Relations Department of the IMF edited the manuscript for publication. Ms. Bonilla also coordinated production of the publication.

The view expressed here are my sole responsibility and do not necessarily reflect the opinions of the New Zealand Government, the Executive Directors of the IMF, or the IMF staff.

I Introduction

The reforms of economic policy and public sector management systems in New Zealand over the past decade have attracted interest internationally. This is in part because the country adopted a comprehensive and comparatively vigorous program of macroeconomic adjustment beginning in 1984 from a very difficult situation that had built up over 20 years or more. The interest also arises because those aspects of the reform program involving the redefinition of the state's role in the economy and social policy, and especially those entailing changes to the Government's own management systems for service delivery, have introduced some innovations not seen elsewhere.

This paper provides an overview of the reforms to the systems of management in the New Zealand Government. It also provides a brief description of the wider context of policy reform, which is necessary for an understanding of why the changes were made. Essentially, the Government saw its own management performance as adversely affecting macroeconomic performance and the achievement of its own priorities. The advice from government officials had incorporated this view since the early 1980s as a consequence of their concerns about the performance of the Government's commercial activities, its investment decision making, and financial risk management. These managerial weaknesses were one of the causes of the unsatisfactory pattern of resource use that resulted in the long-term growth trend in gross domestic product (GDP) per capita being one-half the average of the member countries of the Organization for Economic Cooperation and Development (OECD).

The reform of the system of government management had the following elements:

- moving purely commercial activities from departments into corporations owned by the Government;
- privatization of those corporations in commercially competitive markets;
- structural reorganization of government administration to promote efficiency through competition, providing clear goals and performance information;
- a management framework for central government service delivery that centers on the achievement of detailed performance objectives; and
- shrinking budgets.

These initiatives were all launched by the Cabinet although each required the approval of Parliament. The intent was to exclude the Government from activities it was inherently poor at managing. It was also to improve the management of those tasks which remain the responsibility of the Government.

For those tasks that remain the responsibility of the Government, the initiatives were to establish new institutional frameworks in order to set objectives, to strengthen managers' incentives to achieve those objectives and to use resources efficiently, and to give managers the freedom to manage, but with tight accountability and monitoring and reporting on performance.

Such institutional frameworks are essential features of performance-driven organizations, whether in the private or public sector. They are necessary, but not sufficient, conditions for effective organizations in which high performance is enhanced by constant innovation, concern for service quality, and strategic capability. In government institutions, the crucial additional factors are the capacity for effective strategic policy formulation to set changing goals for organizations, and the leadership skills of top politicians and their professional advisors and managers. The skills of these key actors, particularly their ability to build effective organizations and motivate the people within them, are the essential additional resources necessary for improving the management of government's deliverables.

The reform of New Zealand's government institutions proves these points. The general management frameworks were imposed uniformly on all government organizations, but the resulting changes in performance were variable even though it is accepted that the performance as a whole improved. The highest improvements have been associated with organizational transformations led by effective top managers. On the other hand, there are still, after ten years of reform for state-owned enterprises and seven years for departments, some organizations where the transformation has been limited and performance remains unsatisfactory.

If the New Zealand experience were to be summed up in a sentence, it would be that "good managers cannot succeed in a bad system and bad managers cannot succeed in a good system—both are required to be good."

An account of New Zealand's reforms could be written as a collection of case studies of organizational transformation, success, and failure in management development. This paper focuses instead on the design and implementation of an improved framework of management that was intended to increase the chances of successful transformation of government organizations individually.

There is a heavy emphasis in this paper on the central framework of accountability for specified service delivery, efficient resource allocation and use, external reporting, and auditing. Within these topics, there is a particular emphasis on financial management. These are essential components of a performance-based management system that, in order to meet its objectives, requires a careful balance between management freedom and political accountability. High performance by government institutions and by the Government as a whole will not arise unless there is support from systems that permit the center to formulate and implement strategy, allocate resources in accordance with priorities, monitor performance, intervene in unusual situations, and keep control of macrovariables. Effective modern public administration maintains and strengthens these central functions while releasing managers from the traditional controls that prohibit effective and innovative service delivery.

The International Monetary Fund (IMF) has an interest in the central frameworks of government management, especially systems of financial management, primarily because they have a major impact on economic performance and on the probability that a program of economic restructuring in a country that the IMF supports will be carried out as agreed. The IMF is perhaps less concerned about those issues of management at the level of individual organizations that turn the potential of a well-designed management framework into a reality case by case.

For these reasons, the paper focuses primarily on central frameworks of government management with an emphasis on financial management. The reader should, however, note at the outset that the experience shows that the financial management component of the total system will not, on its own, achieve significant performance improvement at the level of individual organizations, although it can bring major improvements in their budgeting and external reporting. Arguably, there has been greater impact on organizational performance from the systems for setting strategic and operational objectives, empowering managers, assessing performance in terms of results, and appointing and developing senior managers. Good financial management is nothing more or less than an important necessary condition for improved performance.

* * *

Section II of this paper briefly summarizes some key facts about New Zealand that are necessary to put the reforms in a constitutional context for the reader who is not familiar with the country's government institutions. Section III outlines the economic and political background within which the reforms arose. Section IV discusses the problems in public sector management that were seen by the Government at the time, and the theoretical influences on the reforms across the Government as a whole. Section V covers structural reorganization to promote effectiveness and accountability. Section VI provides a short summary of experiences with corporatization and privatization. This is not intended to be a full account of the policies or of the reforms of the individual corporations, which is available in other publications. The section is included because the conceptual framework and the dramatic results were influential on the thinking about reform of core government administration. The scale of the results also had a large impact on the performance of the government sector as a whole, and so must be included for a comprehensive picture of government management reform. Section VII discusses the management system for raising performance in the core of the Government, which is essentially its budgetary sector. It provides the general framework of accountability and performance specification, and introduces the three following sections. Section VIII provides details on recruiting and developing people for senior executive positions and covers some of the industrial relations issues that arose in the reforms. Section IX covers extensively the details of the budgeting, financial management, and accounting regimes for core government administration. Section X draws out some key lessons about the design and implementation of the system for management within the budget sector. Section XI returns to the issues of the implications for New Zealand's macroeconomic adjustment policy and fiscal policy of the reforms of government management systems. Section XII contains some reflections on the implications of New Zealand's experience for other situations.

II Essential Facts

While the fundamental principles underlying New Zealand's government management regime are similar to those of many countries, it should be helpful to a reader to know some essential facts about the country and its Government so that the reforms can be seen within their constitutional context.

New Zealand lies in the southwest Pacific Ocean 2,600 kilometers southeast of Australia. It consists of two main islands and has an area of 270,500 square kilometers, which is similar to Japan or the United Kingdom. The population is 3.4 million, about 80 percent of which is of European origin—predominantly English, Irish, and Scottish, but with people from the Netherlands, Yugoslavia, Germany, and other nations. The indigenous Maori people comprise about 13 percent of the population, and migrants from the Pacific Islands account for a further 4 percent.

New Zealand's GDP per capita is $15,200. Once an agricultural economy exporting to the British market, New Zealand is now a diversified economy. Traditional agricultural exports from the meat, dairy, and wool sectors make up only 43 percent of total exports. In 1960, this figure was 80 percent. Manufacturing now accounts for 25 percent of merchandise exports and tourism contributes 9 percent of total foreign earnings. There has been a similar diversification in the destination of New Zealand's exports—away from the United Kingdom, which once took half of all merchandise exports. Export markets are now diversified with about 35 percent going to Asia, 19 percent to Australia, 15 percent to Western Europe, and 12 percent to North America. Asian markets other than Japan as a destination for New Zealand's exports take 21 percent of the total compared with some 3 percent two or three decades ago. Two-thirds of exports go to the member countries in the Asia-Pacific Economic Cooperation (APEC) group.

New Zealand's constitutional history traces back to the Treaty of Waitangi signed by the Maori and the British crown in 1840, when the country became a colony. It is today an independent state; a monarchy with parliamentary government. Queen Elizabeth II has the title Queen of New Zealand. The Constitution Act contains the rules relating to the transfer of governmental power and establishes the constitutional responsibilities of the sovereign, the executive, the legislature, and the judiciary. There are special requirements governing amendments to this act that have the effect of entrenching its provisions. The Bill of Rights Act protects fundamental rights and freedoms.

New Zealand inherited its government institutions from Britain, and has been described by political scientists as the simplest Westminster-style government in the world. It has a single House of Parliament, with the Government being formed by the political party, or coalition of parties, with a majority of the seats in the House. The electoral laws are undergoing change to convert from a "first-past-the-post" system to "mixed member proportional representation," which will bring coalition government in place of the traditional domination by two parties.

There are no state governments, and the role of local government is largely restricted to urban and rural services that are paid for from property taxes. The central Government is entirely responsible for economic policy and controls all government spending on health, education, and welfare in addition to the conventional functions of a national government. Social policy accounts for approximately 70 percent of the Government's budget.

The Government is run by a Cabinet, formed of members of Parliament belonging to the governing party or coalition appointed either by the party caucus or by the leader of the party, the Prime Minister. Members of the Cabinet are known as ministers. On rare occasions, there are ministers outside the Cabinet. Senior ministers are supported by deputy and associate ministers, who are also politicians in the Cabinet. They are also assisted by parliamentary undersecretaries.

Parliament has several select committees, chaired by backbench politicians. As a rule, they are members of the governing party, but their support for cabinet decisions is not always assured.

The public service is nonpolitical. Heads of government departments are generally career professionals but they must compete for their positions in open competition with people outside the public sector. Appointments from the private sector and from other countries occur. They are employed by the State Services Commission, whose head is appointed by the Government and cannot be removed without the approval of Parliament. This person is usually a professional civil servant.

The Cabinet has a number of subcommittees. Typically these focus on strategy and policy, social services, economic and industrial issues, foreign and defense policy, government administration, legislation, New Zealand's indigenous Maori people, and other matters. There are no civil servants in the Cabinet or its subcommittees, but they appear before the latter to give advice and information on the basis of papers they have submitted. They are required to give open and frank advice to ministers and generally resist pressure from ministers as to what advice to give. Ministers also submit advice to the Cabinet in their own names, and such papers are typically prepared by the minister's personal office staff.

III Political and Economic Background to the Reforms of Government Management Systems

In the last ten years, New Zealand has undertaken perhaps the most rapid and radical reform of economic policy and government management anywhere beyond the former communist countries, Chile, and possibly Mexico. This reform arose mostly out of necessity driven by the need to overcome years of delayed economic adjustment. During this period, every aspect of New Zealand's economic management and government administration has been subject to fundamental review and reform. While in many cases the changes have aligned New Zealand's policies with international norms, or with other countries with a record of innovation in public administration, there are some areas where the New Zealand reforms have taken directions not previously addressed by other countries. These have attracted interest internationally: for example, the development of an independent central bank with explicit objectives for the inflation rate, and aspects of the reform of government financial management and its personnel administration.

In order to understand the context of New Zealand's reform program, it is important to note that it began in 1984 from a situation in which government interventions and controls in the economy were more pervasive and rigid than in any other developed economy. The regime of controls was parallel in significant respects to the control regimes in Eastern Europe at the time insofar as they affected prices, wages, and other incomes. The main features of this control regime are the following:

- Regulations freezing all wages, prices, dividends, rents, and interest.
- All prices and charges for government-supplied services frozen.
- Exchange controls restricting all foreign exchange transactions to items approved by the Reserve Bank of New Zealand—the criteria largely prohibited capital transactions, restricted remittances for current transactions, and ensured export earnings were repatriated.
- Quantitative licensing of imports to preserve the domestic market for local manufactures.
- Extensive subsidies for all major export sectors.
- Tariffs that were very high on items for which there were domestic substitutes and low or zero for intermediate inputs to industry.
- Requirements on financial institutions to hold government bonds at below-market interest rates.
- Prohibitions on public sector pension funds investing in other than government stock.
- Extensive regulatory protection and/or government ownership of the nontradable sectors—transport, energy, communications, finance, construction, and others.

From this starting position, liberalization was the only direction in which policy change could move. The question for debate was how far.

Political Background

Although the National Government under Prime Minister Robert Muldoon had generally relied on direct intervention to pursue its objectives, many of these controls had been in existence only since 1982. In fact, some important steps toward liberalization of the economy in trade and finance had been taken in the late 1970s and early 1980s. By 1982, however, the stabilization of the economy, which had become a serious problem, was the Government's top priority, and some earlier moves to liberalize prices, wages, and interest rates were reversed. The extensive controls were the result of the Government's inability to negotiate an incomes policy with the powerful trade union movement, in its endeavor to control New Zealand's inflation rate. This had accelerated from 10 percent in 1980 to 15 percent in 1982—one of the highest rates in the OECD at a time when major industrial countries were giving high priority to lowering their inflation rates. The Government legislated a total freeze on prices and incomes in the economy in 1982. While this was successful in lowering the rate of inflation in the short term, it created serious problems of suppressed inflation, distorted relative prices, and generated problems for fiscal and monetary policy.

The Government's fiscal deficit rose to 9 percent of GDP in 1982 as a result of several influences. A large cut in personal taxes on lower income brackets was introduced to partially offset the drop in real wages caused by the controls. Further, the regime of controls was supported by policies that fixed the prices of goods and services provided by government-owned organizations at levels that were commonly below costs. Large fiscal subsidies and increased debt were therefore necessary to cover government-owned organizations' trading deficits.

In an effort to create more economic growth over the longer term, the Government entered into a number of very large energy-related industrial development projects. The projects' commercial success depended on the assumption that world oil prices would continue rising at about 3 percent annually in real terms. Most of the commercial risk was, however, left with the Government through various arrangements. Because oil prices did not follow this assumed path, these projects all failed commercially in subsequent years. As a result, $NZ 7 billion worth of debt (10 percent of GDP) had to be taken over by the Government as part of the financial restructuring of the companies concerned.

During 1984, there was growing speculation against the currency, which was seen in the markets as substantially overvalued. The country's credit rating had also slipped from AAA to AA, as international confidence in the economy was eroded. In this volatile situation, the massive defeat of the National Government in an election in July 1984 triggered a currency crisis. This defeat was not merely a reaction to the Government's economic policies; it signaled a complete shift in attitudes toward government in society. The intellectual and political consensus that underlay New Zealand's former prosperity had collapsed.

The incoming Labour Party formed a government that included senior ministers of a younger generation, who believed that the whole direction of New Zealand's economic policy had been wrong. They sought to make fundamental changes to New Zealand's economic and social policies. However, no matter which party had formed the Government, they would have been faced with serious problems in monetary and fiscal policy and would undoubtedly have been forced to relax the unsustainable regime of regulations on incomes and prices. They would also have had to confront a large and rising debt burden and rising unemployment, especially for people with low skills.

The Labour Party, although traditionally socialist, saw the need for radical reforms of economic management and government administration directed toward liberalization of the economy, greater government efficiency, and the reduction of the welfare state. The party's determination to enact reforms was not based solely on the apparent need to respond to the immediate financial and economic crisis; in the long-standing views of some key ministers (the Minister of Finance, Roger Douglas, in particular) the country's economic policies had been fundamentally wrong in some respects for many years. This view was shared by some of the senior economic advisers in the central bank and the Treasury. In addition to recurrent imbalances in fiscal policy and the balance of payments, unstable monetary policy, volatile inflation, and rising unemployment, there was a long-standing concern about the low rate of economic growth. New Zealand's leading economists had been concerned about the growth performance of the economy since at least the early 1960s. Their concern had become widespread through the 1970s and was seen by the Government and its advisers as a critical problem to address through reforms of economic management.

By comparison with other OECD economies, New Zealand had experienced growth that made it one of the worst performers within that group of countries. GNP per capita in New Zealand declined from fifth in the world rankings in the 1950s to twentieth in the 1980s. Had New Zealand grown at the average OECD rate from 1960 to 1985, its income per capita would have been about 50 percent higher at the end of that period. It might be argued that one should make allowances for the fact that higher growth rates may be more difficult to achieve from a high absolute standard of living than from a lower base; and that New Zealand's population grew more rapidly over that period than the OECD average, which required heavy expenditure on social infrastructure. Even so, the relative decline in GDP per capita was a long-standing cause for concern.

Underlying this relative decline was evidence that the productivity of capital and labor was growing more slowly than OECD benchmarks. For some sectors or periods, it may even have been negative, although there are some difficulties with interpreting sectoral productivity measures. Total factor productivity growth as a whole over the 20 years, between 1960 and 1980, was half the OECD rate and one-fifth of Japan's.

Average annual growth in real GDP from 1960 to 1972 had been 3.9 percent, but the effects of the growth rate on living standards had been diluted by a rising population (annual growth in real GDP per capita of 2.1 percent) and by periodic balance of payments problems that caused a "stop-go" pattern. But growth virtually stopped after the boom and bust in the terms of trade caused by the world commodity price boom followed by the first oil shock. As other countries moved beyond the oil shock, particularly some of those in the Asian region close to New Zealand, even more concern arose about New Zealand's apparent inability to make adjustments to changes in its external circumstances.

Growth between 1976 and 1984 totaled only 1.15 percent annually. But the difficulties were not confined solely to growth. Registered unemployment moved from being negligible in the 1960s to 5 percent in the late 1970s, and reached 7 percent by 1983. Annual inflation averaged 12 percent between 1970 and 1984. Later in this period, such little growth as occurred was sustained by a large foreign borrowing program. Government net debt as a proportion of GDP rose from 9 percent in 1976 to 41 percent by 1985, and was forecast to rise much higher because of the large fiscal deficit. In 1992, after the effects of years of unsustainable but declining deficits and bringing onto the books all the off-balance sheet liabilities, this debt ratio peaked at 52 percent.

Economic Background

In the minds of the Government's advisers and of the new ministers responsible for economic policy, the reasons behind this long period of poor performance, which culminated in severe macroeconomic imbalance, are discussed below.

Distortion in the Price System

Generally, it was thought that the government policies summarized above had undermined the allocation of the country's resources by creating disincentives to the channeling of resources toward activities that would lead to higher rates of growth. Through regulations, subsidies, and taxes, the entire price system in New Zealand had been distorted away from reflecting the true value of goods, services, labor, capital, and other resources in the international markets. As a result of these price distortions and poor macroeconomic policy, the development of the tradable goods sector had been suppressed by consequent loss of competitiveness. That is, policies of protection and the allocation of monetary, fiscal, and incomes policies to controlling inflation had led to misalignment of the real exchange rate at the expense of the tradable sectors.

Poor Productivity and Low Innovation

These price distortions had caused the private rates of return on investment in most activities to depart from their social rates of return. Consequently, there developed a pattern of poor resource use, low productivity, and low growth. New Zealand's share of investment to GNP was about the same as in the rest of the OECD, but its growth rate did not reflect the same response. There was particular concern for the dynamic effects of this resource misallocation. Innovation was stifled and misdirected with the consequence that New Zealand seemed destined to continue to drift farther behind the most advanced economies.

Effects of Tariffs and Controls

The very high levels of tariffs and the extensive quantitative controls over imports provided high and widely varying levels of assistance to domestic industry. This had the effect of raising the cost structures of export industries. These problems were compounded by the extensive regulation of domestic industry and the monopolization of many infrastructure activities. Capital markets were heavily distorted through controls on the financial sector, which were intended to channel savings into politically preferred activities. In addition, the entrenched inflation attracted resources into real estate and other activities that provided a hedge against inflation and took advantage of the absence of a capital gains tax.

Inefficient Labor Market

New Zealand's extensive labor market laws, regulations, and tripartite agreements led to wage-fixing arrangements unrelated to enterprise productivity. The laws were primarily directed at issues of income distribution. The Government's incomes policy over the years had led to real wages being higher than could be sustained by productivity improvement.

Inefficient and Inequitable Tax System

The tax system relied heavily on income taxes; the effective rates varied widely and were contrary to generally accepted principles of efficiency and equity in tax design. The marginal tax rate for individuals from middle income levels upward was 66 percent, which produced widespread avoidance—in large part through investments in business proposals that would not otherwise have made sense. The indirect tax system was narrowly based and the tax rates were highly variable. The tax system thus contributed in a major way to the overall picture of a badly distorted price system that was channeling investments away from the highest-value uses of resources.

Excessive Presence of Government in the Production Sectors of the Economy

The Government directly controlled a large portion of the economy through its ownership of enterprises in many sectors of the economy. In some cases, it monopolized them. The Government, through these enterprises, was a major presence in electricity, coal, gas, oil, the postal service, telecommunications, radio, television, road transport, buses, railways, shipping, airlines, banking, insurance, agriculture, forestry, real estate, health, education, science, housing, construction, computer services, engineering, and other activities. Furthermore, all these industries experienced problems of poor management, low productivity, poor service, and poor investment decision making. Well-run businesses were the exception to the rule. All these sectors were imposing unnecessary costs on the exposed sectors of the economy because of their inefficiency, their fiscal effects, and their protection from competition by regulation. These government businesses accounted for 12 percent of total economic activity and 16 percent of national investment, and had a major negative effect on the country's overall competitiveness.

Some Specific Failures in Government-Run Enterprises

In addition to the government involvement in the above-mentioned enterprises, particular difficulties arose from its policy of direct involvement in major new investments in energy and energy-related industries, and its subsidies to various other industries. Huge contingent liabilities entered into when businesses were established became crystallized into actual liabilities to the taxpayers when these activities subsequently failed commercially.

Ineffective Stabilization Policies

As regards macroeconomic policy, discretionary stabilization policies had been badly applied on numerous occasions with the effect of amplifying, rather than dampening, the business cycle. Typically, during the 1970s, the economy was stimulated with fiscal expansion in the run-up to the three-yearly elections, with some tightening after the election but no complete reversal of the earlier stimulus, resulting in a ratcheting effect on the deficit over time. Discretionary fiscal and monetary policy moves had also tended to be procyclical due to the well-known problems of lags in policy formulation. Monetary policy had been neutralized by interest rate controls. Macropolicy lost its effectiveness in stabilization of activity and instead contributed to the deeper problems of low growth by adding instability and risk to markets, while also distorting important price signals.

Evolution of a New Strategy for Development

An integrated approach to macroeconomic policy and microeconomic reform was required in order to raise the country's potential growth rate through more effective resource allocation and improved international competitiveness. At the same time, other national goals of social policy, security, and care for the environment had to be achieved through means that were more in harmony with growth policy. Successive Governments since 1984 have endeavored to achieve these objectives, although, as a Westminster-style parliamentary democracy, New Zealand does not have a formal framework for detailed government economic planning. The broad goals and approaches of the country's development strategy are, however, reasonably clear. An example of an official statement of principles and concepts is contained in a strategy document published with the 1992 Budget.[1] It emphasized the importance of

- stable macroeconomic policy;
- human development;
- openness to the world in trade, finance, technology, and cultural exchange; and
- enterprise and innovation in business and government.

Subsequently, the ruling political party (the National Party) published a strategic vision document based on similar principles.

The scale of the macroeconomic imbalances in New Zealand in 1984, together with the objective of raising the growth rate, presented policymakers with a difficult dilemma. To make progress on both these objectives simultaneously presented problems of coordination of macro- and microreform. The problems of integrating stabilization policy and liberalization policy were the subject of practical experience in a number of countries, and substantial literature emerged on the topic. In particular, some experiences with these issues in Latin America before and around the time of New Zealand's reforms created a precedent that had not gone unnoticed.

While aware of the potential coordination problem, the Government did not want to postpone its program of microeconomic reform while bringing the macroeconomy back into balance. In particular,

[1]Government fo New Zealand, Minister of Finance, *Budget 1992, Economic Strategy B.6* (Wellington), Part II, Annex I.

the scale of the fiscal policy problem did not allow for this alternative, as the fiscal deficit was thought likely to take several years to correct. As events turned out, it took seven years to gain fiscal credibility and the deficit was not completely eliminated until 1994. Also, the microeconomic reforms were essential to improving productivity and reducing the bias against tradable goods. Appendix III contains a schedule of the reforms that were made between 1984 and 1991.

Because two-thirds or more of the 1984 fiscal deficit of 9 percent of GDP was structural, both large increases in taxes and expenditure cuts were required to eliminate the deficit. The effects on economic performance and on the volume of public services would have been large and negative if stabilization had been pursued in isolation from microreforms. The Government also was impatient to progress with its reform agenda, given that New Zealand has a very short electoral cycle of three years. As a consequence, the Government set out to further all its economic objectives simultaneously, hoping that the liberalization of the business sectors and reform of commercial and social activities would boost business confidence and attract private capital sufficiently to offset the short-term depressing effects of rapid fiscal consolidation and tightening monetary policy.

There were some underlying themes in policy design that emerged throughout the program and amounted to a redefinition of the role of the Government in the economy and society. The Government set out to withdraw from those activities in which it does not have a comparative advantage—particularly that of managing businesses. Commercial activities were corporatized and many were privatized. The Government also shed commercial risk that it had previously adopted in various ways on behalf of the private sector. The private sector would be expected to look after itself in a marketplace that would be more open to competition. Over time, this would make the New Zealand economy more internationally competitive.

There was to be a total reform of the systems of government management. Government departments were to provide rising levels of service on shrinking budgets, through increased productivity and more effectively targeting services on those in the community who were least able to care for themselves. The bureaucracy was known to be inefficient and motivated by incentives to grow larger and accumulate influence rather than to deliver services cost-effectively to the people and to innovate for the future.

The reform of New Zealand's extensive systems of social service delivery, as part of its comprehensive welfare state, was based on the principle of abandoning universal provision of services to all citizens regardless of need, in favor of targeting social services on those in need. Also, in some areas, the government monopoly of the provision of social services was relaxed and funding was increased for private sector provision of those services. This implied a major overhaul of tax policy and administration.

Implications for Government and Management Reform

This comprehensive redefinition of the role of government set the following key parameters for reform of management concepts and operations:

- the Government was to withdraw from commercial activity, where competitive markets were established instead;
- remaining government-owned businesses were to be managed efficiently and prudently;
- more complex systems of tax administration were required to administer tax law in an open economy;
- social services were to be delivered in a more targeted way, which was described by some ministers as "fairness on a tight budget";
- there were to be major and rapid shifts in priorities for government spending and service delivery; and
- service levels were to be maintained and improved in quality, while administrative budgets would be cut.

Essentially, the Government was to withdraw from some activities while strengthening its capacity to deliver services efficiently and effectively in what remained.

IV Theoretical Influences on the Approaches to Reform

This section summarizes briefly some of the influences leading to the generic approaches to institutional reform taken across sectors of the Government as a whole.

The Government's aims were to take action to correct the fiscal situation, shift the fiscal priorities of government, and remedy the problems of low efficiency and effectiveness in the delivery of public services. The authorities wished to implement their policy program as widely and quickly as possible. They rapidly became dissatisfied with the constraints of the traditional systems of public sector management in New Zealand on their ability to take these actions. They saw inadequate government management as a cause of New Zealand's unsatisfactory economic performance and other outcomes. The Government also saw that weaknesses in government management were a block to their plans for change. The Deputy Prime Minister at the time, Sir Geoffrey Palmer, expressed the authorities' concerns as follows:

> Effectively the manner in which the public service and State sector generally were organized meant that the Government's ability to shape its own fiscal outcomes was exceedingly limited. . . My own experience was that it was only a determined minister who could control all aspects of his or her department's activities.[2]

Since the early 1980s, official advice had incorporated criticism of the poor quality of public sector management, especially in relation to the performance of government-owned commercial activities, government investment decision making, and financial risk management. It was known that weaknesses in management frameworks had been one of many factors contributing to the unsatisfactory pattern of resource use. There had been costly mistakes in planning of investments in electricity generation leading to massive overcapacity. The railways lacked basic management information. The telecommunications enterprises and postal services made poorly justified investments and lacked information for pricing decisions.

[2]For a full citation see Rt. Hon. Sir Geoffrey Palmer, Memorandum of July 21, 1994, to Dr. Graham Scott.

The new Government had a strong mandate for change, not only in terms of technical aspects of economic policy and government administration, but also from a sea change in New Zealand's politics and wider society. A respected author and political scientist, Colin James, has written about this in his book *New Territory* (1992). He observes that 1984 was a watershed as power passed to a new generation of leaders with backgrounds entirely different from those of leaders of the previous Government, some of whom had served in the Second World War. The Vietnam War-era generation of university-educated professionals led the new Government. Their approach to government was based on different ways of thinking about the issues of government policy.

A process of rapid change in the private sector had resulted from the deregulation of the financial markets, together with the effects of exposing the traded goods industries more to foreign competition, and deregulating protected firms in the nontraded sector. This created a political climate, and even a requirement, for forcing change on the public sector, which had hitherto enjoyed traditional monopolies and protection.

Besides the external pressures for greater effectiveness, efficiency, and innovation in government administration, there were also internal pressures. The detailed central controls over finance and personnel were causing obvious dysfunction in important areas of government administration. The Treasury, for example, was having great difficulty retaining economists, and the Audit Office found it similarly difficult to keep accountants. Senior ministers were complaining about the amount of administrative trivia brought to them for decision. Other ministers were concerned about the dominance of advice by the Treasury; they sought to create a more vigorous and open debate by bringing in other sources of advice.

In the commercial area of government, the new ministers were deeply critical of the financial performance of these organizations and of many aspects of the quality of the services they provided. They were also disturbed to discover the contingent liabilities that accrued to the Government as a result of the earlier energy-related industrial development policies.

In their early attempts to gain control of public expenditure, ministers discovered poor management and financial systems that inhibited their efforts to make cuts and promote efficiency while preserving and enhancing important services. Under the previous Government in the early 1980s, there had been an exercise of across-the-board cuts that had consumed considerable energy, both in ministers and departments, but ultimately it fell well short of its objectives. Subsequent reformers believed the reasons for this failure lay in inadequacies in the framework of management. It was not possible to extract underutilized resources and make productivity gains so that service levels could be met more efficiently. It was too difficult to identify and withdraw the funding for low-priority services.

Following trends in other developed countries, there had previously been a sequence of initiatives for improving the quality of management that began with the introduction of the planning program and budgeting system in the 1970s. Quite sophisticated systems for multiyear budget forecasting had been developed, revolving funds were in use for some commercial activities, and there had been other innovations. However, the philosophical basis was largely that of centralization, so that fiscal control tended to rely on across-the-board measures, together with attempts to impose rules and procedures for resource allocation. Personnel were subject to a sinking-lid arrangement whereby staff members were to be reduced in each agency on a formula basis, with some discretion for reallocating the positions released thereby. There were elaborate rules for compensatory savings, which was an attempt to force existing programs into competition for funds against new proposals.

Capital budgeting was conducted separately from current expenditure, and cost-benefit analysis was applied to major investment decisions. Cost-benefit analysis encountered growing dissatisfaction, particularly because of a tendency for highly uncertain estimates of future events to dominate the analysis instead of a broader approach based on assessing management and financial risk. For example, the Government's support for huge energy development projects was heavily influenced by the assumption of constant 3 percent annual growth in real oil prices. As regards the nonfinancial aspects of management, there were tight central controls on accommodation, stores acquisition, and computer services, and there were detailed rules covering expenditure items.

As far back as 1978, the Auditor General, Fred Shailes,[3] had published heavy criticism of the system of financial management, but those criticisms had been largely ignored by the Government of that time. By 1984, however, there was growing support inside the bureaucracy for change; the Treasury's briefing to the incoming Government included comprehensive criticism of the management systems for central government administration, including the case for reform. This was followed by detailed proposals from that department and the State Services Commission over the coming years.

Influences from Theory and from Other Countries' Experiences

Agency Theory

From the late 1970s, the Government's advisers had drawn on the emerging developments in institutional economics as one source of theoretical insights for developing the concepts behind advice on a new approach to government management in New Zealand. The advisers' interest initially arose from concerns about the dynamic effects of regulation in the private sector, and from the economist Leibenstein's concept of "X-inefficiency."[4] Unsatisfactory experiences in the control and management of government-owned businesses were, however, the first issue where major references to institutional economics and the modern theory of finance were emphasized. A paper by two Treasury officials, Cameron and Duignan (1984), set out a new framework for thinking about institutional structures for creating improved performance by government-owned commercial activities.

The essential feature of institutional economics as it was being developed at the time was that the firm in the theory of economic organizations ceased to be viewed as a production function, as in classical economics, but was instead regarded as a governance structure. In other words, the firm ceases to be viewed as a single maximizing entity and becomes an organizational framework within which individuals transact as participants in an internal market. The theory emphasizes asymmetric information, self-interested behavior within the firm, and bounded ra-

[3]Financial Management and Control in Administrative Government Department, *Report of the Controller and Auditor-General B.1, Summary of Conclusions* (Wellington: Government Printer), Pt. IV, p. 7, 1978.

[4]Harvey Leibenstein, *General X-Efficiency Theory and Economic Development* (Oxford: Oxford University Press), 1978.

tionality, meaning that individuals seek to optimize their position, but within a framework of imperfect information.

It follows that the Government's problem is one of contracting efficiently between principals and agents in a way that minimizes the so-called "agency costs" of setting up and monitoring that contractual relationship. Theories based on these concepts are known as agency theories.

From this perspective, the practice in New Zealand of making strategic decisions at the central political level for major government-owned commercial activities after drawing on advice from the organizations themselves, was seen as a deeply flawed institutional structure for assuring the ultimate owners of these businesses—the taxpayers—that resources were efficiently used. While a theoretical perspective assisted in the development of new approaches, it was scarcely necessary in order to observe the problems of the traditional approaches.

From this dissatisfaction emerged New Zealand's state-owned enterprise model, based on the principles that emerge from agency theory. The theory of finance was also influential in thinking about establishing the financial structures for the state-owned enterprises and designing the regimes for monitoring managerial performance.

Institutional economics also played an important role in the design of the framework of management for central government departments. Here the problems of contracting for performance and controlling transactions costs were exacerbated by the absence of numerical measures of output. A framework for solving the contracting problem had to be developed that did not rest heavily on the assumption of precise measures of output, but nonetheless through various systems and processes could create an environment more driven to achieve results. This theory emphasizes the importance of "private ordering" or "social capital." These are the established values, norms, and conventions that provide implicit agreements, incentives, and restraints on individuals within complex organizations as they go about their business. It had long been commonplace in private sector business management to emphasize the importance of culture, and later leadership, in successful organizations; the institutional theorists were increasingly giving attention to these issues.

As in the private sector, institutional economic analysis of the public sector is concerned with selecting governance structures that minimize transactions costs between the parties involved in the production distribution of a service. While the underlying forces are assumed to be the same in both sectors, the way in which they emerge in the public sector is unique. In the private sector, governance structures emerge from the competitive process so the superior ones survive and the inferior ones die. In the public sector, a successful governance structure is one that survives the competition between competing coalitions of legislators for votes. There are transactions cost problems of a major kind throughout the relationship between legislators and citizens and they have no parallel in the private sector. It is for this reason that governance structures in the private sector should be imported into the public sector only with caution and attention to detail.

Because public sector agencies find their justification within this larger context of the relationship between citizens and legislators, it is not uncommon to find features of those agencies that seem inefficient, in terms of not appearing to take the lowest transactions costs available, while still being consistent with transactions costs minimization in the wider constitutional relationship. This phenomenon explains, for example, the appearance of self-imposed restrictions on the powers of legislators over their administrative agents. Such constraints can strengthen the credibility of commitments to citizens concerning the likelihood of succeeding governments revoking policy commitments. Institutional economics theories of government assume that citizens are rational and forward looking and consider the present value of the benefits and costs of government decisions over time. This approach underlies the theory of institutional choice in the public sector as advanced, for example, by Horn (1995, p. 23).

While the business literature is generally not grounded in theory, it was influential in the thinking of New Zealand's advisers because of the weight of evidence and the widespread conviction among business writers that hierarchical systems of management control had become a major cause for organizational failure in the private sector. It seemed obvious that the same corrosion was likely to be at work in the hierarchical institutions of government. At a practical level, many private sector management techniques were introduced into government agencies beginning at this time. The experience tended to confirm this view of the causes of poor performance and thereby increase the pressure for reforms. It was generally found that there was nothing fundamentally different between the private and public sectors when it came to the practical details of more effective management.

Public Choice Theory

This theory was influential in thinking about redesigning public administration. It seemed plain that there were problems of "provider capture" in major areas of public service provision, and various frameworks were proposed to correct these through increased transparency, changing organizational structures, and contestability in the provision of services.

New Accounting Methodologies

By the time the reforms were under way in the late 1980s, there was an emerging literature in accounting that emphasized a positive methodology, and, in particular, drew on agency theory to develop hypotheses about the relationship between governance arrangements and the financial reporting systems that arise within them. This literature was helpful in assisting in the development of government accounting standards that, in one or two places, departed from the standard conventions of the generally accepted accounting principle. It helped analyze, for example, the accounting information that was appropriate to the governance structure established by the State-Owned Enterprises Act.

An account of the theoretical influences at work during the earlier years of the New Zealand government reform program is found in Scott and Gorringe (1989).[5] An IMF working paper written by a Treasury official, David B. Heymann (1988), while seconded to the IMF, also shows the direction of thinking by officials at the time.

The experiences of other countries were influential on the New Zealand program at a number of points, although the specific details of most policies differed from events elsewhere, sometimes in important respects. U.K. policies for the corporatization and privatization of industry had an influence, as they did elsewhere around the world. British and Australian experience in expenditure decision making at Cabinet level provided some valuable lessons. Both countries had considerable success at times in the 1980s in controlling government expenditure through well-focused and tightly managed Cabinet decision-making structures and procedures. Australian budgetary processes and documentation and also financial reporting provided a precedent for some of the changes that were made. For example, the *Australian Forward Estimates* document presented to the Parliament in Canberra was viewed as being a world leader in several respects.

[5]G. Scott and P. Gorringe, "Reform of the Core Public Sector: The New Zealand Experience," *Australian Journal of Public Administration* (March 1989), pp. 81–92.

Generic Frameworks for Institutional Reform

While the details of reform in each organization of government were driven ultimately by practical issues in politics and administration, the influences described above and the need for rapid change led to the emergence of generic approaches to reform of the basic structures of governance and accountability. These approaches varied from sector to sector, but, at the general level, had in common some simple and basic principles underlying the development of constitutional frameworks and processes:

- establishing strategic directions and clear organizational objectives;
- defining the roles and accountability of responsible parties—Parliament, ministers, appointed boards, central government agencies, and line managers;
- developing information on service delivery, resource management, and financial situation;
- defining roles and processes for monitoring performance;
- providing incentives for high performance and aligning the interests of managers with the objectives set for organizations by ministers and other responsible authorities; and
- delegating authority to managers to empower them to manage.

Scott and Gorringe (1989) and Scott, Bushnell, and Sallee (1990) explain the theoretical basis of these principles and the common threads running through the reforms of different parts of the Government. Translating these general principles into specific frameworks of accountability and authority led to a variety of detailed institutional approaches to cover different classes of organization. These were

- fully commercial trading activities—mostly headed toward privatization;
- commercial enterprises intended for permanent government ownership;
- natural monopolies in government ownership;
- corporate enterprises in social service delivery with mixed commercial and social objectives;
- statutory organizations beyond the day-to-day control of ministers; and
- core government departments responsible to ministers and overseen by Parliament.

The following sections elaborate structural reform to implement these principles in different areas, and their application in commercial activities and in central government administration.

V Structural Change to Promote Effectiveness

Since 1988, the great majority of government agencies engaged in noncommercial activity have been substantially restructured. The underlying detail is vast and is beyond the scope of this paper. There are clear patterns in the approaches taken to restructuring departments. Such patterns were adopted with more or less variation throughout the whole body of government administration, although it would be exaggerating to say that there was a generic model of reform that was generally applied.

Basic Features of Reform

The basic features of the restructuring are described below and illustrated by reference to the general policy objectives and frameworks in a number of areas.

Separation Between Policy and Operation

Policy advice was separated from the operational units responsible for the administration of that policy. In practice, administrative agencies are expected to provide advice and their practical experience is valued, but it was seen as undesirable to have the Government's advice on policy and resources coming primarily from parties with a direct interest in the service delivery.

Separation Between Funding, Purchasing, and Provision of Service

The funding for public services was separated from the purchasing and provision of those services, with a view to creating arm's-length contractual arrangements between the Government's roles as funder, purchaser, and provider for specified services to both the Government and directly to the public. In some cases, this involved creating specialized purchasing agencies one step removed from the Government's executive decision-making processes. This scheme was installed in the provisions of health and science services. In education, the funding is provided directly to the educational institutions by grants on the basis of student numbers. In housing, the funding is provided directly to the public in a voucher-type arrangement to purchase services from government agencies or the private sector.

Competition Between Service Providers

To provide pressure for efficiency and effectiveness, the structures provided for actual or potential competition between government-owned providers of public services and also between government providers and private sector providers. This required the removal of monopoly protection for government providers, and the introduction of pricing systems that established the full resource cost of government-provided services.

Reallocation of Responsibilities Between Government Departments

To promote more effective management, the allocation of responsibilities between government departments was subject to intense scrutiny. The objectives were to group similar functions; avoid conflicts of interest; and disassemble conglomerate organizations that had shown themselves to be difficult to manage, lacking focus, and given to concealing information internally—information that the restructuring was intended to expose. The structure of government departments has important influences on the flow of information to central coordinating bodies, the Cabinet, and Parliament. The decisions on particular structures involved trading off a number of influences such as information flows, efficiency in production of services, coordination, decision making, and accountability. In designing the structure of advisory agencies, the reforms were guided by the principle that the Government has a particular role in making trade-offs between conflicting community values such as wealth, security, equity, environment, and civil rights—particularly of indigenous people. It was felt that the structure of the advisory services should broadly reflect these values in order to promote more effective decision making and reconciliation of value conflicts.

Examples of Reform

A few examples of structural reform will illustrate the extent to which these general principles emerged in practice in the government departments dealing with education, health, housing, science, transportation, justice, and land.

Education

Until the late 1980s, New Zealand's school system was based on central administration from the Department of Education through local education boards, which, in turn, controlled the individual schools. Zoning was enforced, so that pupils had to attend the school in the area they inhabited. Parents had no effective say in the running of schools. The system was reformed by removing the zoning regulation and essentially funding schools on a per capita basis according to the number of pupils they enroll. There are a number of special grant programs to accommodate schools with particular needs. The governance of the schools was passed to elected boards of parents. Due in part to pressure from the teachers' unions, the reform stopped short of delegating all the authority for personnel management to the schools. Provisions were made for new schools to be formed by groups of parents. Although there was still a strong bias in favor of state schools in the funding arrangements, there are policies for providing a degree of support for certain private schools.

Further information on these reforms can be found in the Report of the Taskforce for the Review of Education Administration (1988) (Picot Report) and Ministry of Education (1988).

Health

From a system of government bulk-funding by the area health boards, which were run by a combination of locally elected representatives and central government appointees, the Government put in place a funder-purchaser-provider split. Hospitals were corporatized into Crown health enterprises. The Government's funds were passed over to regional health authorities, run by government appointees who write purchase contracts for services either from the Government's own hospitals or from private sector providers. Purchase agreements between the Government and the regional health authorities establish purchasing guidelines that follow national health policies and priorities. A committee of advisers has been appointed to determine the core health services that the Government will publicly fund for all citizens, leaving services outside that core to be provided by private medical insurance and other mechanisms. A full description and comment on the health reforms are contained in Appendix V.

Housing

One corporation had been responsible for managing the stock of housing owned by the Government, and provided assistance to people who needed housing by rationing those houses. Other benefits were available for people who could not obtain state housing, but the system had a strong bias toward government provision of housing assistance. The corporation also lent money on concessional terms to qualifying buyers of houses. The corporation had a predominant influence on housing policy advice going to the Government until a restructuring beginning in the late 1980s and continuing when the National Party was returned to Government in 1990. There had, however, been other sources of advice available. Under the reform, the corporation was set up on a commercial footing with the objectives of managing the stock of housing commercially, although it was clear that the corporation was also intended to take note of certain social objectives. The broad intention was also that the rents on government houses should rise to market levels, while assistance to people with housing needs would be distributed directly by the Government. This was achieved through finance that could be spent by the recipient on either public or private housing. The bias of assistance toward tenants of state houses was removed from the late 1980s on a phased basis. The portfolio of mortgages of approximately $NZ 2 billion was sold off. Further information on these reforms can be found in the New Zealand Ministry of Housing (1991).

Science

Prior to the reforms, government supported scientific research through budgetary funding for scientific units within various government departments, and, in particular, one large Department of Scientific and Industrial Research. These units had tended to be resourced incrementally within the budget process, and various attempts over the years to impose priorities and introduce incentives for effectiveness had not been judged unsuccessful. The reforms split all the science-providing units out of their departments and reassembled them in corporations very similar to state-owned enterprises, but termed Crown research institutes. It is not intended that they be privatized, but they are intended to act commercially in their dealings with the private sector, where they are free to enter into joint-venture arrangements and other commercial activities. It had not been appropriate to transact commercially from within the budgetary sector of the Government as the attendant commercial risks could not be managed effectively.

The funds that had been allocated to these organizations were pooled; a Science Foundation was established by the Government to dispense these funds to the Crown research institutes on a contracting basis in competition with other providers of scientific research services from both the public and private sectors. A Ministry of Science and Technology was established to provide advice to the Government on the overall science policy of New Zealand. On its advice, broad priorities are established for the foundation. This has been accepted as a more effective way of setting science priorities than the previous corporate planning of the Government's science establishment. The reforms have brought about less duplication of effort and efficiency such as the sharing of expensive equipment, as a result of the commercial disciplines and the tight, although not shrinking, government budget. One of the institutes failed to secure sufficient funds for financial viability and was closed. The structure of the new system can be seen in Figure 1.[6]

Transport

The Ministry of Transport had been a large conglomerate department with responsibilities in policy advice, administration, regulation, and service provision. It controlled a special traffic police force, the meteorological service, air traffic control, civil aviation policy, and air accident inspection, and had responsibilities in relation to road safety, maritime transport, and other matters. From a peak of over 4,000 employees, this ministry has shrunk to a payroll of 60 today, while its component parts have been placed in organizational forms appropriate to their function. In particular, several commercial corporations were established, the traffic police were combined with the general police force, and some regulatory functions were passed to the Ministry of Commerce, while the ministry itself adopted a coordinating and policy advisory role. The reform of transport has been accepted as a considerable success and a model of restructuring to promote effectiveness. As part of the transport reforms, a division of the now-abolished Ministry of Works and Development, which was responsible for road construction and maintenance, was established as an independent organization named Transit New Zealand which now dispenses all the government funding for roading. This puts it beyond the patronage system that once influenced those decisions. Further information on these reforms can be found in New Zealand Ministry of Transport (1993).

Justice

One of the last major conglomerate departments to be disassembled was the Justice Department, which was responsible for prisons, courts, the conduct of elections, various policy advisory functions, and registries of information such as births, deaths, marriages, and landownership. In 1995, the Government implemented the results of an enquiry into the reasons for unsatisfactory performance, one of the reasons being that the department was too unwieldy to be managed effectively. It recommended that a Ministry of Justice be created to provide advice and policy coordination over the spectrum of justice issues. The operational activities were allocated to newly created departments to administer the courts, prisons, and other activities.

Land

Some functions were transferred to other departments where there was a natural fit of activities. For example, the land registry system was brought together with the Department of Survey and Land Information. Also in 1995, the Department of Survey and Land Information was disassembled into two parts: a department responsible for oversight of the land title system (land titles are guaranteed by the Government) and a state-owned enterprise selling surveying services to that department and other customers in competition with a small private sector surveying industry.

Commercial Regulation

The regulatory functions of many government departments that related to their own service delivery or specific sectors of the economy were relocated into the Ministry of Commerce, in the belief that general regulatory frameworks and policies should be developed with a view to the public interest as a whole rather than to the interests of particular sectors or providers.

Assessment

A comprehensive assessment of the impact of structural reforms on performance has not been con-

[6]For further information on these reforms, see Science and Technology Advisory Committee, "New Zealand Science and Technology New Deal" (Wellington), 1988, and "Report of the Ministerial Science Taskgroup" (Wellington), 1991.

Figure 1. Organizational Structure of the Science System

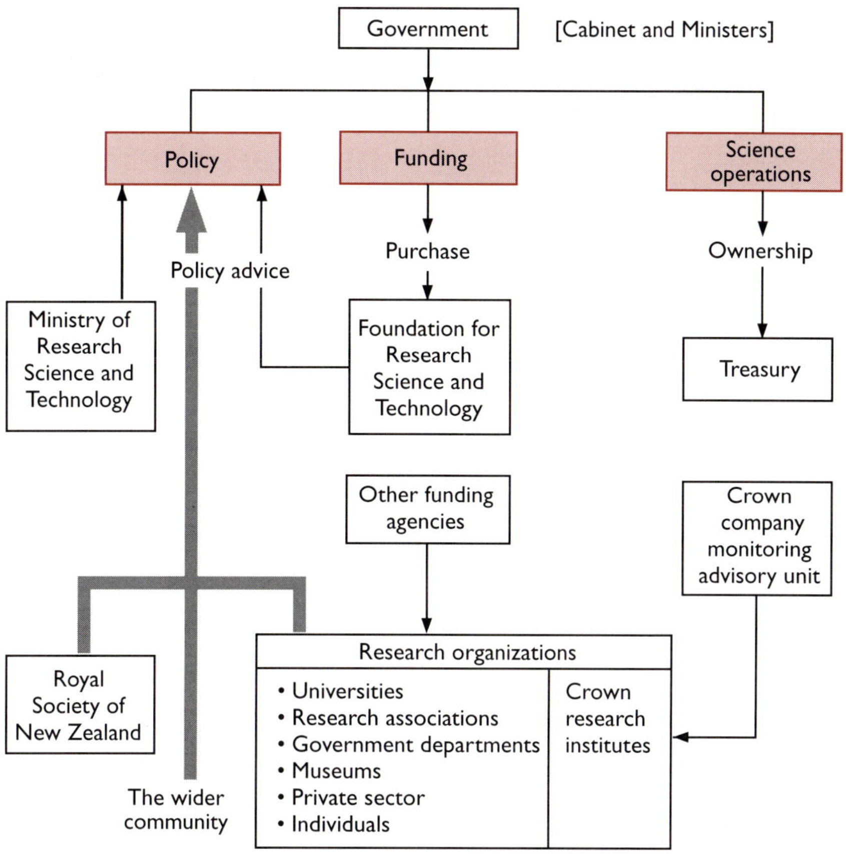

Source: *The Science System in New Zealand,* Ministry of Research Science and Technology (August 1994).

ducted and would be very difficult to accomplish methodologically. There are a large number of case studies of structural change but it is difficult to isolate the contribution of structural change on its own from the other changes going on simultaneously. Structural change has demonstrably been associated with performance improvement in numerous cases. This is clearly the case for all the Government's commercial activities, where the structural reforms involved a completely new form of governance and new objectives and freedoms. The performance improvements are described in the next section.

For government departments, the association of structural change with performance improvement is clear in most instances, but not universally so. Evidence from the Ministry of Transport and other large departments clearly supports a judgment that performance is improved by creating focused business units. Focused units have the advantage of being able to provide much more clear information about their resource use, as the separation forces the allocation of assets to specific activities. It is thereby easier to generate information about the real costs of services.

There have also been performance improvements in departments that have had little structural change and there have also been ministries restructured out of existence, such as the Ministry of Works, whose presence has not been missed by ministers generally.

Further case studies need to be done to form deeper judgments about the sources of performance improvement in departments, but the conclusions set out below are reasonable on the basis of experience.

Conglomerate departments, that is, those with a range of distinctively different kinds of activities, are inherently difficult to manage to high standards of performance. Breaking them up into their component activities permits clear specification of objectives and the specialization of the management on specific issues and processes involved, with short chains of command.

The separation of funding, purchasing, and provision of services leads to observable changes that are thought to promote better management. Table 1 contrasts an integrated organization containing funding, purchasing, and provision of services within a single management system with the separated form.

The integrated organization is more prone to capture of policy and funding by the large provider interests. Also, agency costs are likely to be high by comparison with the disaggregated form because of difficulties in striking and monitoring contracts. The organization's objectives are multidimensional and often in conflict so that performance specification and monitoring are difficult. Also, both sides of the contract are working in the same organization, and staff internally have incentives to do well inside the organization as a whole, probably through promotion into central administration.

Management information systems in a conglomerate tend to be serving many masters, and a lot of information would form part of an explicit relationship if contracted between independent organizations that become buried in internal management decision making and that therefore are often poorly documented. Because of the attenuated lines of communication, central management is likely to be at an information disadvantage compared with people in delivery units, who are closer to clients, which complicates the task of performance specification and monitoring.

The above-mentioned scenario is likely to create dead-weight losses through slow-moving management and distortion policy and resource allocation. If it is a monopoly situation, the incentives for customer service will also be weak.

The controls on management discretion exercised from the center are typically the application of general controls rather than designed to be part of effective contracts between the parties. This restricts the ability of the providers to manage more efficiently and effectively because they are subject to controls that are part of a general regime of accountability to politicians.

Contestability

The points discussed so far would apply whether there is competitive service provision or competitive purchasing or whether monopoly provisions apply to the separated form as well as the integrated form. Conceptually, the integrated form could also be subject to competition, although in practice, this rarely occurs (e.g., competing health maintenance organizations).

Adding competitive pressures to the separated structural approach can make a major improvement in performance through reducing agency costs and the stimulus and threat of competition for business. The major illustrative cases involve monopoly funding agencies (science, health, and education), so there is scant evidence of the impact of competition on funders. Competition among providers for the funds clearly is keeping them under continual pressure to seek improvements in terms of producing

Table 1. The Case for Structural Separation of Funding, Purchasing, and Provision of Services

Integrated	Separated
Multilayered hierarchal management • Remote leadership • Information flows distorted and concealed • Performance goals hard to define and conflicting • Homogeneous hierarchal management	Flat structures • Leadership closer to customers • Management information requirements easier to define • Clearer performance goals • More specialization in staffing
Conflicting objectives resolved internally	Clear objectives and transparent trade-offs
Diffused incentives for client service	Clearer provider focus on client service
Central management controls	Delegations and freedoms
Confused accountability	Clearer accountabilities
Direct political governance	Appointed boards over providers with goals set by legislature
Provider capture of policy and funding advice through internal management	Providers must make a public case for their views against independent policy advisors and funders

outputs that are more efficient and effective in achieving desired outcomes. A competitive process generates benchmark information and contracts that are negotiated against the background possibility of the purchaser switching to an alternative provider. The experiences of the health reforms demonstrate that hospitals are finding new ways to contain costs and are exiting lines of business for which they cannot compete with lower-cost providers—for example, rest home care for the aged.

How Much Disaggregation Is Enough?

Contracting has its own costs, and excessive fragmentation can weaken the ultimate accountability of the Government to its constituents. Coordination problems can, after a certain degree of disaggregation, become difficult. Large organizations tend to be more efficient not only where there are economies of scale, but where services are inherently difficult to define clearly in relation to performance goals; there are large investments in specific capital that is not easily diverted to other uses (including human capital); or there is a great deal of uncontrollable uncertainty surrounding the possible outcomes. In these circumstances, integrated organizations relying on management processes can be superior to arm's-length contracting. New Zealand may have reached the limits of wholesale disassembly of organizations if the views of some of the present most senior politicians are an indication.

Problems are seen to have emerged in areas where the components still have to coordinate over policy development, information exchange, relationships with common clients, and other matters. Experience shows that a lot of informal contact that occurred naturally in a unified organization has to be established by much more deliberate, if not necessarily formal, means to ensure that the big picture is not lost in pursuit of focused organizational objectives.

This is not to suggest that there is evidence that the informal contact in the larger organizations produced better coordination and strategic thinking. Some critics of the changes argue this way, but there is as much evidence to suggest the reverse. The experience does support a conclusion that a deliberate and continuing effort is needed to ensure that the decentralization of activities for better service delivery is accompanied by development of central capabilities to generate longer-term strategy, advise on and review the effectiveness of policy, set performance objectives for operating units, and monitor their performance.

Government Ownership of the Providers

Government ownership of provider organizations has tended to be concentrated in areas of the economy where there are real or perceived reasons why the pursuit of a profit motive by the provider might be inconsistent with government goals, which go beyond the simple questions of price and quality of service. The most common of these issues is the question of access, where the Government is concerned with who gets the service and is not prepared to allow market forces to determine that. Government ownership also arises, however, in relation to services where there are inherent difficulties for consumers in identifying and reflecting their own best interests in their purchases. Health and education services are, for these reasons, sectors where government ownership persists because of fears by the populace reflected in the views of politicians that control through ownership mechanisms.

In effect, the Government remains able to impose certain requirements on the boards and management of provider organizations that are not necessarily consistent with strictly commercial objectives. For example, the Crown health enterprises are required to be concerned about various public health goals, and all government-owned enterprises are required to show a sense of social responsibility—undefined.

Government ownership of both the purchaser and the provider side of a contractual relationship presents the Government itself with a conflict of interest that can be quite difficult to resolve. The pressure to avoid the embarrassment of heavy losses from bankruptcy in government-owned providing organizations by manipulating the purchase decisions in their favor are difficult to resist. The separation of the responsibilities for purchase and ownership in the hands of separate ministers has generally worked out, although there are built-in tensions between, for example, the Minister of Crown Health Enterprises and the Minister of Health, over whose portfolio is called on to support a hospital that cannot break even with the revenue from its contract with the regional health authorities.

Complex Contracts

In the gray area between the circumstances in which structural separation offers real benefits and where it clearly does not, the focus is on trying to evolve the design of complex contracts. The term "relational contracting" has emerged as a way of capturing this idea. This is occurring in 1996, particularly in health, where there are a number of difficulties regarding short-term price and volume contracting. On the other hand, the funding of public interest scientific research and in housing policy, the contracting is much simpler and generally more effective. Over the whole of the New Zealand public service, the move toward contracting out a lot of services has occurred relatively easily largely because it has been left to public service managers to make their own decisions as to what to contract out and what to retain. They have done this subject to budgetary pressure and it has generally tended to occur in areas where the conditions for successful containment of agency costs apply.

Changing Managers

New Zealand's experience with restructuring of government organizations suggests that one of its major influences on performance improvement comes from the opportunities it creates to introduce new management. There are examples of structural changes where the existing managers retain all the top positions and there is little change in performance. Transforming a department with a culture of compliance and avoidance of risk and innovation to a high-performing organization requires a major change in that culture, which will only occur if it is modeled by top managers committed to the change and embedded by them through their daily activities. Generally this requires new management, but not always.

VI Reform of the Commercial Activities of the Government

Historical Background

By comparison with other OECD countries, New Zealand Governments had historically assumed a major role in the provision of traded services in addition to an extensive involvement in administration and social services. At the beginning of the reform period, almost one-third of the labor force was employed in the public sector widely defined (e.g., this includes education, health, and local government).

There are a number of historical reasons why the Government was so heavily involved in commercial activities. In key sectors of the economy, private companies, usually in financial difficulty, were nationalized. Before the Second World War, others arose from the control of natural resources such as coal, oil, and gas. Others involved monopoly provisions of services to the Government itself, such as computer services and accommodation. In the finance sector, there were large organizations providing finance on a nonmarket basis to key sectors such as farming and housing. Arising from the historical development of New Zealand, the Government has a huge presence in land and forestry. Public ownership of utilities was the normal pattern through central and local government. Public enterprises contributed 12 percent of GDP and 17 percent of gross investment (one estimate puts it as high as 20 percent). Below is a summary of government commercial activities as of 1984.

Extent of Government Involvement

The New Zealand Post Office ran the postal network (which was the country's largest transportation system) and the telephone and telecommunications network (by law the only telecommunications system allowed in New Zealand), as well as a large retail bank.

Apart from the Post Office Savings Bank, the Government was deeply involved in the finance sector in other ways: it owned the largest bank, an investment bank, two large pension funds, and a huge fund to compensate people for any losses they might suffer in earthquakes.

Most of the country's electricity system, including coal, gas, geothermal, and hydroelectric power stations, surface power transmission lines, and the undersea cable connecting the country's two main islands, was run by the Energy Ministry. The Government was deeply involved in oil exploration and aspects of refining.

The largest farmer in New Zealand was the Government, through its Lands and Survey Department. The largest single owner, grower, and planter of forests in New Zealand was also the Government, through its forest service.

The country's largest coal mining company was government owned, as well as a large civil engineering and construction business.

The Government was also deeply involved in the transportation sector. It owned and operated the only railway system; Air New Zealand, the country's only international and largest internal airline; and the largest fleet of passenger buses.

The Government also ran large numbers of other businesses within government departments: the air traffic control system, a printing office, a large computer agency, and the country's largest insurance firm, to name a few.

At the local government level, essentially all public utilities were in public ownership including transport, water, waste disposal, gas, and electricity distribution ports and airports. Some local governments owned forests.

These trading enterprises took a variety of organizational forms. Many were government departments, some were public corporations operating within the state service employment laws, and others were public corporations operated outside those laws and limited liability companies under private sector commercial laws whose shares were owned by ministers.

Starting in 1985, the Government set out to reform these activities with a view to removing their heavy fiscal loads from the Government's finances and increasing their contribution to the economy by being more efficient. Given the size of these government businesses in relation to the economy, their inefficiencies had a major negative effect on the country's overall competitiveness in international trade. There was not only the direct effect of their poor performance on government finances and on their customers, but also the cost excesses and lack of innovation following from their privileges and protections.

Throughout all these industries, there were problems of poor management, low productivity, poor service, and poor investment decision making. This system produced what the Deputy Prime Minister in 1986 called "massive economic waste."[7] Well-run businesses were the exception to the rule. The following are examples:

- It often took about six weeks to have a telephone installed, and, several months were required for installation of multiline corporate telephone exchanges—a substantial disadvantage for businesses trying to compete in an open international marketplace.
- There was too much capacity in electricity generation. The state coal mines had made losses in 20 of the previous 22 years, and were mining coal that was difficult to reach while ignoring coal that was easier to exploit.
- At one airport, money was spent to install an air traffic control system that was not needed and was later dismantled.
- In 1986, the number of staff at the Post Office Savings Bank had grown by 75 percent in ten years, while the bank's business had shrunk in size by more than one-third.

Besides these long-standing government enterprises, the Government in the early 1980s had a policy of direct involvement in major new investments in energy and energy-related industry, and also subsidized various industries. This generated contingent liabilities to the taxpayers when, later, many of these activities failed commercially. By 1987, $NZ 6 billion of these liabilities had crystalized. It also led to extreme pressure on the long-standing policy of applying a 10 percent real discount rate in the cost-benefit analysis of government projects, and this was seen to have failed as a safeguard against poor investments. The need for a new approach became obvious.

Causes of Poor Performance in Government Businesses

There were a number of reasons for the problems of ineffective resource use in government businesses. Below are a few examples.

[7]Rt. Hon. Sir Geoffrey Palmer, "Directions for State Enterprise, Purpose Performance and Profit, Redefining the Public Sector," *Proceedings of the 1986 Convention of the New Zealand Institute of Public Administration* (Wellington), pp. 25–31.

- Confusion developed between commercial, social, and political goals. This undermined the direction of the businesses.
- Conflicts of interest for managers arose through their role in advising the Government on budgets and regulation policies that directly supported the businesses they managed.
- No effective accountability for results was placed on either managers or politicians.
- No information was available on the performance of the businesses in terms of customer satisfaction or return on assets employed.
- The pricing, regulatory, and tax policies that cushioned the businesses meant that private investment in these sectors was either prohibited or noncommercial and precluded any comparison with private sector performance norms.
- Managers had very little freedom to manage. The central control of personnel and finance by the Government made effective management impossible and created incentives to grow bigger and to avoid or delay innovation.

State-Owned Enterprise Framework

The growing influence of modern institutional economics during the late 1970s and early 1980s led to a new approach to thinking about the Government's control of business enterprises. In this approach, and as noted in Section IV, the problem of efficiency in state-owned enterprises is analyzed in terms of transaction costs, information, and incentives required to encourage the business to act in the public interest. A particular focus is placed on the relationship between the Government as owner on the one hand, and the managers as its agents in running the business on the other hand. A framework for corporatization was developed that, in theoretical terms, was intended to deal with this agency problem in corporate governance through clarification of roles of the parties, clear commercial objectives, good information, performance monitoring, and a fully competitive market environment. This framework was based on the following principles, which the Government announced in 1985.

- Noncommercial functions are to be separated from trading functions.
- The principal objective is to be run as successful business enterprises.
- Managers are accountable to ministers for agreed performance and free to make all management decisions.
- Enterprises are to operate without competitive advantages or disadvantages.

• Boards of directors would be established on private sector lines using commercially experienced individuals.

In 1986, the State-Owned Enterprises Act was passed with the following objective:

> to promote improved performance in respect of government trading activities and, to this end, to (a) specify principles governing the operation of state enterprises; (b) authorize the formation of companies to carry on certain government activities and control the ownership thereof; and (c) establish requirements about the accountability of state enterprises and the responsibility of ministers.

The act also required that these enterprises operate as successful businesses, which were to be (a) as profitable and efficient as comparable businesses that are not owned by the Crown; (b) good employers; and (c) organizations that exhibit a sense of social responsibility by having regard to the interests of the community in which it operates by endeavoring to accommodate or encourage these when able to do so.

There is an explicit provision for the enterprises to be required to provide noncommercial services by the public directions of the Government and with separate funds provided.

The directors appointed to the first state-owned enterprises were of a high standard and not aligned politically with the Government.

The Government's responsibility for managing risks and returns on resources invested in the companies was assigned to a minister, the Minister of State-Owned Enterprises, who had these responsibilities across all the Government's commercial investments, and no responsibilities for policy issues within the sectors of the economy in which the companies operate. For example, the Minister of Energy does not control the Government's shareholding in the Electricity Corporation.

State enterprises are formally created by being included on a schedule to the Act. The first nine state enterprises were created in 1987. Two years later, there were 15, and this number more than doubled following the wave of reforms in science and health after 1990, described below. The implementation usually involved forming an establishment unit, typically headed by the person who is to be chairman, who sets up a company that negotiates purchasing the assets from the Government and arranges to take over the staff that will be needed. Typically, this involves redundancy and sometimes redundant workers are taken over by the company to be dealt with under the rights pursuant to New Zealand's labor laws. In some cases, the companies only took over the staff they needed and left the redundant workers with the Government.

Performance Objectives and Accountability

A Statement of Corporate Intent is the key document establishing the accountability of directors to the shareholding ministers. For each corporation, on an annual basis, this statement lays down the scope and objectives of the business; performance targets and financial ratios; accounting policies and performance information; and dividend policies.

The corporations are monitored on behalf of the shareholding ministers by the Treasury and a specialized monitoring unit that is headed by a senior official with an established record for business analysis in the private sector. The companies are audited by the Auditor General, who may subcontract the work to a private sector auditor; and the companies are also examined by a select committee of Parliament. An account of the state-owned enterprise policy, with details of each of the businesses involved in the first wave of corporatization, is contained in Duncan and Bollard (1992).

Results of the Reform

Throughout the corporations, dramatic improvements in customer service, lower prices, and higher returns to shareholders were produced from some of the major enterprises over the transition period (Chart 1).

Electricity prices fell 13 percent and costs 25 percent. Unit costs fell 28 percent, gigawatt-hours (gwh) per employee rose 71 percent, and profits rose 187 percent.

The productivity of telecommunications rose 85 percent and prices fell 20 percent. The waiting time for a telephone fell from six weeks to two days. Since privatization, the waiting time has fallen further, to one day. A study of the distribution of the static efficiency gains between shareholders and customers, by de Boer and Evans (1994), shows that the larger part of the gains accrued to the customers by a substantial margin. The study states that

> the bulk of the efficiency gains have accrued to consumers and that the most of these stemmed from price reductions on 1987 consumption levels. Telecom, as the producer, has fared less well. Price reductions transferred producer surplus to consumer surplus, and the productivity gains and output expansion have not been enough to offset the transfer. Implementing the capacity-adjusted productivity gain does not materially affect the conclusion. The size of the total gain to society is

Chart 1. State-Owned Enterprise Outputs
(Real price indices)

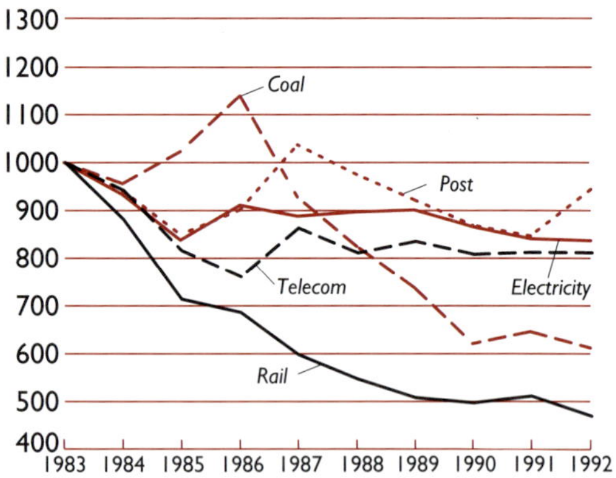

(Base 1983 = 100)

Source: State-Owned Enterprise Unit.

quite significant. Indeed, at a discount rate of 10 percent total gains are of the same order of magnitude as the original sale price of Telecom in 1991. . . .[8]

The New Zealand postal service had productivity gains of 12 percent and turned a $NZ 38 million loss into a $NZ 43 million profit. Staff levels fell 30 percent. Under a memorandum of understanding with the Government, the price of a standard letter was to rise no faster than the consumer price index, although the corporation was forced to absorb the full costs of the introduction of a 10 percent goods and services tax (GST). In fact, prices have been kept below inflation, and nominal prices have been cut. From 1987 to 1995, the real cost of a standard letter fell 33 percent, and New Zealand now has the third-lowest postal rates of OECD countries and is one of the two lower countries that has regulated and subsidized prices.

Rail freight rates dropped 50 percent and a $NZ 77 million loss became a $NZ 41 million profit. The company has now been privatized, generating $NZ 400 million, and further gains are expected.

In the coal industry, tons per employee grew 30 percent while real prices fell 20 percent. The workforce was halved while output increased.

Forestry Corporation staff numbers were cut by 65 percent over three years, although many former workers set up businesses with the assistance of the Corporation and contracted with it for services. In the last year as a department, there was a government injection of $NZ 70 million, followed by a turnaround in operating surplus, after adjusting for differences in activity, of $NZ 100 million in real terms in the first year. By 1990, after-tax profits were $NZ 138 million.

The port companies formed by the harbor boards, as required by central government legislation, cut the workforce by 50 percent. Prices dropped by between 20 percent and 50 percent, and turnaround times for ships declined—for example, by 56 percent at the port of Tauranga.

These new corporations have been far more successful commercially than the previous government-owned businesses, some of which had spectacular collapses in the wake of the world stock market crash. The Bank of New Zealand is the most notable, and twice required recapitalization. The new frameworks of accountability and monitoring of government corporations highlighted the inadequacies of the previous approaches.

Duncan and Bollard's detailed study of 14 enterprises documents marked improvements in commercial performance coming from better definition of core activities, aggressive marketing, contracting out to reduce fixed costs, rationalization of investments, and staff reductions.

Fiscal Implications

While no summary data exist on the net fiscal impact of government businesses prior to corporatization, the situation was summed up by the Minister of Finance's comment prior to corporatization that the Government derived no return from $NZ 20 billion in assets. By contrast, in 1992, the state-owned enterprises were paying $NZ 537 million in dividends, equal to one-tenth of the revenue collected from GST. The state-owned enterprises paid sums of a similar order in taxation.

Implications for Labor

The first round of productivity improvements relied heavily on reducing staff directly employed by the enterprises. The workforce fell 50 percent over the eight enterprises in the Duncan and Bollard study (1992, p. 55). Generous redundancy payments were made for a few years. Some enterprises, particularly in the forest sector, promoted the contracting of work to firms established by former employees. In the telecommunications industry, the emergence of competitors provided job opportunities for some

[8]David de Boer and Lewis Evans, "Government Department to Public Corporation in a Deregulated Economy: the Economic Efficiency of New Zealand Telecommunications," Victoria University of Wellington, Graduate School of Business and Government Management, pp. 21–24, Revised August 3, 1994.

former employees. There has been no comprehensive study of the employment histories of people made redundant by state-owned enterprises.

Second-round effects are not quantifiable because the feedback effects on the remainder of the economy of the improvements in efficiency in the state-owned enterprises, through micro- and macroinfluences, are likely to have been overwhelmed by more powerful effects on the demand for labor from movements in the terms of trade, macroeconomic policy, technology, and other developments with influences on the labor market.

New Issues in New Zealand's State-Owned Enterprise Policy

This first phase of corporatization involved placing businesses in the hands of generally competent boards and skilled and motivated managers. The second phase, beginning in the late 1980s, was the privatization phase. It was realized that these healthy infant enterprises, and some of those that were not so healthy, had no more reason to be in public ownership than many of New Zealand's private sector companies. They were hungry for the capital, technology, management, and commercial freedom that they were inhibited from acquiring in public ownership. Any national development goals the Government had in relation to the companies could be better met by comprehensive policies that affected public and private enterprise alike. Privatization proceeds so far have amounted to about $NZ 13 billion, and the sale of major forest assets will add significantly to that sum.

New Zealand's experience with state-owned enterprises showed that significant gains were made by corporations, but that governance problems remained difficult. There was a fear, and some evidence, that the gains would erode over time because the pressure to perform and innovate is generally weaker where the Government is the owner. Overall, the costs of public ownership outweighed the benefits, and, indeed, in many cases, it was seen that there were no benefits.

Privatization was therefore begun, giving, as expected, a second wave of improvements in customer service and in returns to shareholders. Total asset sales as of the end of 1991 amounted to $NZ 13 billion, or roughly 16 percent of GDP. The privatization policy sought greater efficiency and innovation, but also fiscal benefits from paying off government debt with the proceeds, and avoiding the need to support business expansion with further capital injections. Businesses were generally sold in the open international market to single buyers, in order to receive payment at a premium for control of the companies.

The third phase of corporatization under the national Government after 1990 had the following new features.

- The creation of corporate forms of organization in health and science has expanded the number of entities to be managed, although many are small.
- Boards of Crown health enterprises and Crown research institutes, and Housing New Zealand (the new corporation established to manage the Government's housing assets) have been set both commercial and noncommercial objectives. The Government does not intend to sell these organizations.
- A complex tangle of ownership and regulatory issues has arisen around those publicly owned businesses that are natural monopolies in the general sense of the term.
- Permanent ownership of these enterprises by the Crown removes the possibility of passing the problems of governance and management to the private sector after the gains from corporatization have been achieved. Their complex objective functions, resulting from the mix of commercial and noncommercial objectives, have been imposed by means that are not as contractually transparent as the State-Owned Enterprises Act intended. This geometrically adds complexity and cost to the processes of management and shareholder monitoring. Very difficult issues in asset valuation, governance, and regulation have arisen around natural monopolies, in particular the national electricity distribution system.

Theory and experience suggest that efficiency is likely to be sacrificed in the pursuit of multidimensional goals or at least greater political control. A heavy reliance on the personal motivations of managers and boards to act in the public interest seems inevitable as the incentive framework to do so will not be powerful. It is hoped that this quality pertains to the 400 board members who will be required to run all these entities.

Who Benefited from Corporatization in New Zealand?

A systematic study of the distribution of the benefits of corporatization has not been done, and would be very difficult methodologically due in part to the problem of establishing the counterfactual. It is, for example, improbable that staffing levels in large departmental businesses could have been maintained even if they had not been corporatized. The substantial proportion of the economy's resources employed in these businesses, the indirect effects of their activities, and government protection of them on the rest of the economy meant that corporatization also had macroeconomic feedback effects that altered the distribution of benefits. Their productivity improvements certainly had a direct impact on the international competitiveness of New Zealand's industry through, for example, the large reductions in the costs of transporting bulk commodities across the waterfronts mentioned above.

The productivity improvements listed above speak for themselves in general terms. There were reductions in prices, improvements in services, and taxes and dividends greatly increased, often moving from losses to profit for the first time. At the same time, there were typically large staff reductions and restructuring of staff establishments, wages, and conditions of work reflecting reduced penalty payments, more flexible job descriptions, and staff deployment, reduced middle management layers, and more emphasis on pay for performance. In terms of the change in factor shares, the pattern is more variable and reflects the influences of factors specific to each industry. Case studies of telecommunications and electricity discussed below illustrate this point.

Telecommunications

Corporatization brought large efficiency gains to the Government's telecommunications business. The telecommunications sector of the former Post Office Department employed 25,000 people prior to corporatization, and by the time of the privatization, this number had fallen to 16,000. (Since privatization, it has fallen further to 4,000, and is planned to go still lower.)

The old department invested heavily, but with considerable inefficiency. At the time of corporatization, it was revealed that large stocks of obsolete capital equipment had been accumulated and never used. This was probably the consequence of the system for central investment appraisal by the Cabinet Works Committee and the end-of-year spending spree that was encouraged by the cash-based appropriation system for controlling departmental spending.

After corporatization, the company launched a major spending program to modernize the phone system over three years (by 1990). After privatization, more stringent criteria were imposed on investment spending.

From an initial balance sheet with a net equity of $NZ 3.6 billion after restructuring in 1988, the value of the business to the Government rose to $NZ 4.25 billion at the time of sale in 1990. Since privatization, this figure has doubled.

The 20 percent real drop in prices and major improvements in quality and speed of service made customers clear winners, and volumes demanded rose sufficiently to permit revenues to rise 10 percent a year even though the economy was essentially flat.

From 1988 to 1990, the Government benefited from $NZ 441 million in taxes and $NZ 443 million in dividends, and from the sales profits. These are potentially augmented by the incipient capital gains tax payable by institutional investors and share traders on their share of the approximately 5 billion of increased share value since privatization.

The personnel costs fell from $NZ 451 million to $NZ 382 million over the three years, showing that the gains were not only from cutting labor costs.

Overall, the picture is of a company in a dominant, but not entirely monopoly, position that passed the efficiency gains to the customers and to the Government. It is of interest, however, that calculations of the economic value added, that is, excess return over the Government's cost of capital, show that the return did not turn positive during the corporatization phase. It has done so since privatization.

Electricity Corporation of New Zealand

At the time the Electricity Division of the Ministry of Energy was corporatized, there was an unresolved debate over the proper valuation of the assets for purposes of transfer to the new company. Central to the argument was the issue of future price assumptions to be used in calculating the cash flows from low-cost hydro stations. There were many views regarding how to assess long-run marginal cost, and whether it would be the basis of future pricing. The issue was finally resolved by an arbitrary political decision, which tends to cloud any judgment in the adequacy of the rate of return, as the value of the asset base is uncertain.

The transmission system was split off from the generating company and, although it was once planned to have it owned by a club of users, it has been established as a state-owned enterprise. This is in conflict with the original principles of the state-owned enterprises policy, as it has created a monopoly that is not readily subject to competitive pressure. It is potentially subject to constraint by the general competition laws administered by the Commerce Commission and the courts.

This issue of price setting for power continued to dominate the affairs of the company that remains in government ownership. The company endeavored to raise prices in 1991 based on its view that new investment in generation was needed and it could not be justified at current prices. A parliamentary inquiry and pressure from the Government forced the company to back down, which created the situation that the future path of prices was assumed to be politically influenced. At the same time, the need for new investment was becoming more apparent.

The Government and the industry is well advanced in creating a competitive market in electricity, which will have the great advantage of allowing a range of views about the price necessary to support long-run investment to emerge. While the corporation saw price increases necessary to support new investment, it is likely that the emergence of a market will introduce efficiencies in both electricity supply and demand that will drive perceptions of the long-run marginal cost below what the corporation's perceptions have been. In 1996, the Government split the corporation into two competing generating companies, having earlier split the transmission assets off into a separate company in order to promote competition.

Without the development of a market, it was unlikely that new generators would enter the market, and the Electricity Corporation's monopoly would continue. This monopoly is one of the main reasons that the earlier price interventions were justified. The threat of interference in prices will be lessened as the market develops and new generators enter the industry. The market company now comes under the jurisdiction of the Commerce Act, which means it is dealt with under competition policy and is at arm's length from politicians, even though government corporations had a close involvement in establishing it.

The key point from these developments is that the distribution of gains from corporatization and the potential for further gains has been, and will be, determined by the Government's regulatory policy and its approach to developing the industry. It intends to remain the owner of the dominant generators and may therefore continue to exert influence on the pricing and investment strategies of the corporation.

A few insights can be gained from looking at the main indicators of who has benefited from the corporatization thus far. From the customer's viewpoint, real average wholesale prices fell by 13 percent over five years. The share in the total energy market rose from 43 percent to 50 percent. From the owner's viewpoint, the combination of falling prices and increased sales resulted in revenues rising slowly about 2 percent a year. The margin (net operating profit after interest and tax) fell slowly from 56 percent to 46 percent; capital employed was roughly constant until a large increment in the last year, when the Clyde Hydro Station came on stream. Dividends were pushed from an initial $NZ 60 million to $NZ 200 million a year, and the number of staff decreased from 4,154 to 2,861, although there had been substantial cuts of about 2,000 in the transition from being a department.

The overall picture is of a monopoly firm operating in a stable state with constant prices, healthy margins, and making strong returns to the Government both in taxes and dividends.

Short-term gains have been shifted to the customer through political influence on prices that may not support the investment in new capacity under the current institutional arrangements. As noted above, the long-run marginal cost of electricity is likely, however, to be lower if a market develops, so that a wider range of sources of supply enter the market to compete with the corporation, and conservation measures can compete on an even footing with generation.

Clearly, the opportunity existed for the Government to allow the price increases to go through, in which case, the return to the Government would have been higher. There was a precedent for this in the late 1970s, when the Government raised electricity prices by 50 percent all at once.

Government as Owner of Monopolies

The electricity case demonstrates that the Government as the owner of a monopoly has the discretion to use that monopoly to the benefit of customers, or its own revenue or wealth. The Government has the same discretion as a private owner of a monopoly in this regard. It raises the question of how Government should best exercise or restrain its powers as the owner of a monopoly.

Dividends and Reinvestment Policies

Governments have generally preferred cash dividends over leaving profits to the enterprises. It might appear that the Government milks the corporations for cash as a contribution to fiscal policy, but there is more to it. The Government does not want corporations to enter new and risky areas of business. This no doubt reflects a view inherent in New Zealand's state-owned enterprise policy, since the beginning—that the Government is a poor manager of commercial risk. The early experiences of the major energy-related government-supported investments in the early 1980s and the subsequent collapses of the Bank of New Zealand, the Development Finance Corporation, and the Government Property Services clearly support this view.

Government ownership of businesses presents an inescapable dilemma for the Government. It is hard to resolve this dilemma other than by privatization, which has been the preferred option for businesses where there are no strong grounds for government ownership for noncommercial reasons.

If its enterprises are in competition with private organizations that are managing business risk more adequately, then the latter will steadily drive the government companies out of the market. If the Government allows its companies to take major risks, but the governance structures and incentives inherent in government ownership mean that it will on average manage that risk less well than its competitors, then it will also eventually be driven out of the market. A logical conclusion is that the Government should not own businesses in competitive areas of the economy, and should take a cautious attitude to approval for its businesses extending the scope of their businesses. The corollary of this is that businesses pass their excess funds back to the owner rather than expand into new ventures at or beyond the margin of the activity the Government wants to own a business in.

The possibilities for avoiding a repeat of the disasters of the early 1980s lies in the direction of strengthening the governance structures associated with government ownership, making the functions contestable to strengthen the pressure to manage well and expose performance information, and ensuring that staff are skilled and motivated personally to manage the businesses in the public interest. The difficulty in doing this over time for all businesses (in New Zealand, the Government needs 400 directors to run all of its enterprises) is one reason why privatization is the preferred policy in relation to businesses for which there is no overriding noncommercial reason to preserve government ownership.

Economic Value Added as a Technique to Enhance State-Owned Enterprise Performance

The economic value-added (EVA) method pioneered by Stern Stewart is used in a growing number of areas in both the public and private sectors in New Zealand. This is an innovative use of the old concept of opportunity cost applied to the use of capital. The method's advantage over traditional accounting methods of measuring return on funds employed is that it establishes a benchmark for the cost of capital employed in the firm around which the rates of return actually generated by management are compared. If the actual return is less than the cost of capital, then the capital should be withdrawn and put to better use elsewhere. If the actual returns exceed the cost of capital, then this margin can be used as a basis for assessing the performance of management in adding value for owners.

The cost of capital is calculated by adding to a risk-free rate of return, usually the Government stock rate, a premium for risk of investment in equities in general, which is adjusted by a measure of specific risk normally associated with the industry it is in, by comparison with the equity market as a whole. This measure of the cost of equity is then averaged with the cost of debt finance for the company using the debt-equity ratio to provide a weighted average. While there are endless complexities surrounding this simple formula drawn from the capital asset pricing model, it does produce an estimate of the opportunity cost of capital employed in an activity that is widely accepted in financial markets as the relevant measure.

As Stern Stewart states, all business decisions can be thought of as falling under four headings.

- Operating the business to increase the rate of return on capital;
- Building the business to increase capital if the rate of return exceeds the cost of capital;
- Harvesting the business to withdraw capital if the rate of return falls short of the cost of capital; and
- Reducing the cost of capital by reducing the premium for the various business and financial risks in the hands of management.

As a basis for monitoring the effectiveness of management, extra value produced in excess of the cost of capital can be broken down into elements that are within management control and outside management control. While the boundary between the two is blurred, it does make a difference as to whether, for example, profits in the Government's forestry business arise from a world boom in wood prices or more effective management of forests.

The system is used for improving the specification and assessment of performance in state-owned enterprises. Where the Government has a monopoly position of mixed-commercial and noncommercial objectives, unusual difficulties arise. Driving managers to increase the returns from a monopoly position mentality means raising prices to extract the rents from the monopoly position. The key is to separate out the actual or potentially competitive activities where competitive pressure is real, and place them within the EVA regime. Noncompetitive activities cannot be driven by financial performance measures alone and must be supplemented by other performance targets.

Implications for Regulators

If the market is not competitive enough to ensure efficient management, then the standard regulatory solutions are available, although in some cases, EVA may contribute to a solution. The problem for the Government as owner and the managers of a monopoly business is to decide whether that position should be used to extract super profits through monopoly pricing and if not, how to ensure continual productivity improvements and appropriate pricing. Traditional approaches gave regulators the role of setting prices in order to provide a fixed rate of return on assets. The use of a formula to fix prices that imposes a requirement to have prices decline in real terms is one approach to the problem of overcapitalization and low productivity improvement within the traditional approach.

An alternative is to constrain the owner's rights to take abnormal returns from exploiting the monopoly by fixing that return by reference to benchmarks from related industries. Managers are then encouraged to strive for productivity improvements that are not assessed in terms of profits above normal. This is being implemented in New Zealand, and taken furthest in the Airways Corporation, which is responsible for air traffic control and other airport services. The company reports its performance on an EVA basis with the constraint that it is not aiming to drive that significantly above the cost of capital. It sets out its standards of service performance in terms of prices and various technical indicators.

The EVA approach simulates others in that it is sensitive to the valuation of the business, which determines the capital tied up. The standard view is that optimized deprival value is the appropriate approach. This seeks to devalue assets that are not what would be installed today below their depreciated historic cost and to approximate an opportunity cost approach. This view is subject to much litigation and debate in New Zealand, where the court has ruled in a case involving Wellington Airport and the airlines to the effect that a discounted cash flow method of valuation using existing prices set by that natural monopoly is superior to a valuation based on marginal cost pricing that effectively writes down past investments. It would be surprising if this principle were to become entrenched as it is not in the public interest that government natural monopolies use their power to impose the costs of past mistakes and obsolescence on their customers.

Conclusion

While a general equilibrium study has not been done, the New Zealand case experiences strongly suggest that there were major gains in efficiency from corporatization that were distributed among customers and owners. The movements in real prices and service levels show that customers were major beneficiaries of the changes.

The swing from making no returns to the Government as owner and making constant demands for subsidies, to making substantial payments in dividends and taxes meant that citizens as owners were a major beneficiary also.

The state-owned enterprise model was designed and implemented with the expectation that the distribution of the effects of its efficiency gains would be made as if it was a private sector business. Deregulation of product and factor markets and removal of privileges was essential to this.

Privatization has also emphasized deregulation to ensure competitive market pressures. Some of the remaining businesses in government hands have dominant positions and some are natural monopolies. The basic state-owned enterprise framework does not itself solve the essential monopoly problem that was left to the application of general business regulatory policy. They are, however, subject to more intensive scrutiny and exposure of their decisions than private sector businesses.

The creation of government businesses (not under the State-Owned Enterprises Act) with mixed commercial and social objectives and the natural monopolies in some areas, for example, airways and electricity transmission, present new challenges. Theory and experience suggest that the approach to businesses should involve recruiting superior boards and management, enhancing monitoring, encouraging government determination not to extract rents from its natural monopolies, establishing techniques to enhance contestability, and exposing real economic performance information and privatization, where the preconditions for efficiency are met.

VII Management for Improved Performance in Core Government Administration

In 1988 and 1989, the Government of New Zealand passed legislation that endeavored to lay the foundation of a management framework for its departments and other government-controlled noncommercial entities, based on the principles of management discussed in Section IV. This entailed

- clarification of strategic and operational objectives;
- clear specification of the roles of the parties in organizational governance;
- resources allocated on the basis of the results being sought;
- decentralization of management authority with accountability for results;
- incentives for performance; and
- information about results achieved and the condition of the organization.

The measures reflected the widespread dissatisfaction with the previous regime. There were concerns to ensure that the effectiveness of government spending on public services was increased and the efficiency of their production enhanced. The measures took shape against the backdrop of an excessive and persistent fiscal deficit, and the prospect of years of stringency in controlling the growth of this form of government spending.

Key ministers believed that they were called on to undertake too many decisions about details of departmental expenditure that should have been left to departmental managers. In particular, ministers were involved in industrial relations issues to a greater degree than they thought appropriate. In 1985, remuneration increases in excess of 20 percent for some classes of public servants were negotiated directly by ministers. Although this pay rise followed a pay freeze between 1982 and 1984, the increases were viewed as excessive, even at the time, and subsequently caused difficulties for macroeconomic stabilization.

Concern also grew that the bureaucracy was not sufficiently responsive to changing government priorities. Having been out of power for nine years, ministers were concerned that the civil service would be slow to respond to new policy priorities.

Ministers also sought major improvements in performance by departments. The enormous improvements in efficiency and quality of service that were resulting from the transformation of the commercial activities of government departments following the State-Owned Enterprises Act led advisers to search for a framework that would bring analogous incentives for efficiency to the activities of other government entities and departments.

On the other hand, departmental managers were frustrated with the extensive controls over all aspects of personnel, finance, and other matters, and were well disposed to the idea that they should accept more accountability and loss of permanent tenure in exchange for the freedom to manage with much greater responsibility and discretion.

Previous System

Prior to the reforms of the management of government institutions that began in the mid-1980s, financial management systems in the New Zealand Government had the following elements:

- A program budgeting system.
- Appropriations expressed as cash for inputs into programs.
- Central control of disbursements by the Treasury, although the capacity of central data processing services had become constrained and large departments had been given delegated authority to write their own checks. Departments generally kept bank accounts for a small proportion of the total funds they were appropriated, but most of their checks were written by the Treasury on receipt of vouchers authorizing the payment.
- Use of the fund accounting approach as the structure of the Government's financial records and reports. The structure comprised a consolidated fund, loans fund, loans redemption account, trust fund, and roads fund.

• Detailed instructions issued by the Treasury that controlled all departmental spending on a line-item basis and allowed very little discretion to managers to vary their input mix.

• All investments, down to quite modest sums, were required to be approved by the Cabinet. Larger items were subject to a requirement for a positive benefit in a cost-benefit analysis employing a 10 percent real discount rate (although the analysis was not always completed satisfactorily and often overridden by political judgments).

• Application of this departmental financial management framework to large commercial organizations as well as to administrative cost centers (as discussed in Section VI)—for example, the postal service and all electricity production.

• A corporate planning process that was applied with considerable variation in quality, and that generally did not express the business goals of organizations satisfactorily.

• A budget cycle based on adjusting the cost of existing policy for inflation, and then adding the cost of new policy proposals. Arbitrary rules attempted to force some of the funding for new policies to come from compensatory savings in existing expenditure programs.

• Three-year forecasts of departmental spending were prepared (although not always published), but fiscal decision making took place entirely on an annual basis.

• Controls on the use of computers, including a requirement that departments use a government-owned central bureau service; on accommodation; and on numerous other inputs.

• The State Services Commission had control over staff numbers in departments and administered a detailed array of occupational classes that governed pay level gradings and promotions.

• Salaries were fixed centrally, with a special commission setting top salaries.

This system had come under heavy criticism as early as the Auditor General's report, noted above, in 1978, because it lacked clear objectives and any accountability for results or useful information about effectiveness and efficiency. There were attempts at reform, but no political backing for significant change.

By the mid-1980s, ministers and their advisers viewed the problems of core government administration as follows:

• The objectives for the departments were not clearly specified.

• The respective responsibilities of politicians and civil servants were confused, so that lines of accountability and responsibility were never clear.

• The structures of the departments lacked focus and grouped functions in ways that undermined performance. Information was suppressed and cross-subsidies between different activities were concealed, in some cases, deliberately, but in most, simply as a consequence of the system. There were conflicts of interest—for example, departments giving advice about the regulation of activities in which they were directly involved—and this lack of focus in the structures weakened incentives to perform effectively.

• Accounting systems did not measure total resource use by excluding, for example, the cost of capital and depreciation of assets and liabilities for employee pensions. The systems created incentives for poor resource use; costs were not accumulated in a way that enabled assessments to be made of the costs of departmental outputs; and information about risks, assets, and liabilities was ignored or distorted; for example, the impact of interest rate changes on the costs of servicing government debt was included in the deficit, but the effects of changes in exchange rates on the value of the debt was not. This led to undesirable borrowing in low-interest rate, strong-currency markets.

• The control systems administered by central agencies curtailed freedom to manage effectively, leading to poor central decision making about matters that could have been managed more efficiently in a decentralized way. These control systems generally destroyed incentives to perform.

• There were few sanctions for poor performance. The system was designed for microcontrol of inputs rather than performance in the production of effective public services.

• Ministers were making detailed decisions about the internal management of departments for which they did not have adequate knowledge and suitable incentives. They saw these decisions as the proper responsibility of departmental managers.

In harmony with the principles behind the reform of government commercial enterprises, a system was designed that sought to resolve these problems through establishing clear objectives, allocating responsibility to managers to achieve those objectives, giving managers the freedom to adjust inputs in the pursuit of output performance, and giving managers information about the achievement of outputs and the efficiency of their resource use.

Roles, Accountability, and Delegation

Under this new system, the position is that the minister, acting within the collective responsibility of the Cabinet to which he or she belongs, is now formally responsible for specifying the performance requirements of the departmental chief executive responsible for service delivery. Decision-making authority about how to meet those performance requirements is passed to that chief executive.

There are now incentives to perform, and requirements for performance information. This simple scheme is shown in Figure 2 and was implemented by two acts of Parliament: the State Sector Act and the Public Finance Act.

The State Sector Act passed in 1988 clarified the roles and responsibilities of ministers and chief executives. This act, together with the Public Finance Act, which was passed a year later, enabled the development of annual performance agreements between the two parties. The agreements specify what is to be delivered, and expectations of quality and cost, together with management objectives for ensuring efficient use of resources. The act provided for departments to be headed by chief executives in place of the former permanent heads; a five-year contract term with tenure based on performance was established in place of the previous permanent tenure.

The chief executives were made the legal employers of the staff in their departments. Previously all staff had been employed by the State Services Commission. This adjustment gave the chief executives powers to hire and fire, set salaries, and negotiate conditions of employment. (Their financial delegation under the Public Finance Act are discussed below.)

The contract of employment of chief executives is a formal legal contract subject to the normal provisions of New Zealand's labor and contract laws. The essential principles underlying these laws are concerned with equity and due process. The contract prescribes the determination of remuneration and the manner in which performance objectives will be set and recorded in a performance agreement and the process for assessing performance. The contract also establishes obligations on executives to act in accordance with the values and ethics of the civil service and to be concerned with the wider collective interests of the Government, in addition to serving the minister of the day.

The performance agreement concept took several years of experimentation to perfect, and will no doubt evolve further. At the time of writing, it establishes for each chief executive the key results expected for the year, the chief executive's priorities, the schedule of departmental outputs to be delivered, his or her obligations with regard to maintaining and building the capacity of the department for the longer term (the ownership objectives are discussed below), and any personal development goals for the chief executive him- or herself (Box 1).

Figure 2. Accountability Relationship

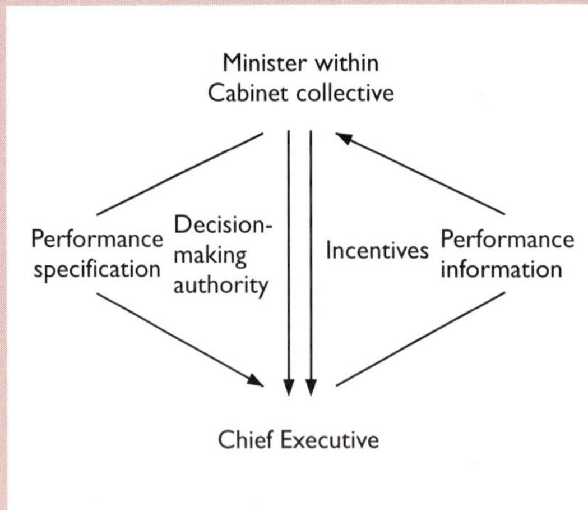

Elements of the performance agreement are discussed below.

Emphasis on Ex Ante Performance Specification

The accountability relationships between ministers and chief executives were seen to be more effective when ex post monitoring, assessment, and reporting were based on clear ex ante agreements about performance expectations. The effect of this reform was to make much more explicit the relationships between ministers and chief executives, involving as it did the prior specification of the service to be delivered by a department during a forthcoming year. In this respect, the system differs from those operating in many other jurisdictions, where a much greater effort goes into ex post evaluation than ex ante specification. The New Zealand system was based, in part, on the belief that problems in performance assessment arise more often from inadequately specified objectives than from the ex post evaluation itself. Ex post evaluation is in any event of limited use for purposes of accountability without the prior agreement on objectives with the person being held to account.

These concepts of ex ante performance management became a determining factor in structuring other elements of the management system, including the chief executive performance agreements, departmental corporate plans, appropriations, and departmental budgets, and ex post financial and performance reporting. By this means, the various elements of the system came to reinforce one another, being structured by reference to the

Box 1. Chief Executives' Performance Agreements

- Between ministers on behalf of the Government and chief executive of a department.
- Key results area: commitments to strategic objectives linked to the Government's strategy.
- Output requirements or purchase agreements.
- Management requirements or ownership agreements.

same principle of performance management and accountability.

Setting Objectives to Shift Control from Inputs to Outputs

The focus for the management system was *outputs* rather than *inputs* (as in the previous system) or *outcomes* (as advocated in much of the literature on public sector management). See Figure 3.

Outputs and outcomes are formal concepts defined in legislation, and the distinction between them is critical to the concepts of financial appropriation and accountability. Outputs are the goods and services produced by departments or third-party suppliers. Outcomes are the consequences for the public resulting from the outputs and activities of government. The purpose of government activity is to produce desired outcomes.

Introducing modern management techniques into the public sector required the removal of extensive webs of controls over internal management decision making and the use of inputs. A method was needed for permitting freedom from these controls while still ensuring that politicians, and ultimately Parliament itself, had control over the disposition of public funds. It was decided to adopt the output concept.

Fundamentally, an output is anything that can be contracted for by the department or agency as the supplier and the Government, or third parties, as the purchaser. Outputs should be individually unique, internally homogeneous, and capable of being costed, and not involve a large element of overlap with other outputs. It must also be evident whether or not an output has been delivered. As in the private sector, the character of any product or, in this case, output, can be simple or complex. In the public sector, they are usually complex, and the process of contracting for their provision must take account of the complexities both of the service and of the manner in which it is produced.

Figure 3. Outcomes, Outputs, and Inputs

Outcomes	Benefits sought by the Government (Strategy and operations)
	↑
Outputs	Goods and services produced by departments
	↑
Inputs	Resources used to produce outputs

The more complex the service, the more involved the relationship between purchaser and provider. For example, soil tests for farmers by the Ministry of Agriculture are done by having the farmer send in a soil sample in the mail; the results are returned on standard forms. There is no need for discussion between the purchaser and the provider. At the other extreme, complex policy advice is presented to ministers in a continuing dialogue with departmental officials. As each piece of advice is unique in some respect, there is a heavy emphasis on the track record and reputation of the advising department and the people within it. The process is the same as that prevailing in the private sector when comparing the different relationships between purchaser and supplier involved in selling, for instance, soap on the one hand and investment banking advisory services on the other. This point is discussed and illustrated in Heskett, Sasser, and Hart (1990, p. 36).

The essence of the output approach is that one party is taking responsibility for the delivery of the service and another for specifying the services required. In practice, the provider will be making suggestions and giving advice about the services required, while the Government, as purchaser, will want to be informed about some aspects of how it is being produced, but the system rests on this fundamental underlying distinction between the roles of the party.

The more precision used in the description of the outputs, the greater the control by the Government over the allocation of its resources, and the greater the likelihood that this can be done in terms that are relevant to its objectives, especially when compared with a resource management system based on a control of inputs. The Government, in fact, believed that its extensive controls over inputs were not giving it effective control and that its budgets were being driven by the inertia in the system rather than by responses to change in priorities and demands for greater efficiency. Although much traditional control was given away in the reforms, overall experience showed that effective control had been increased. This depended crucially on careful and detailed specification of outputs.

The starting point was in 1989/90, when the first set of outputs was debated between the central agencies and each department, and then reviewed by ministers. Every government department had to prepare a document that listed all the outputs they were funded to produce grouped into homogeneous classes, and with estimated costs, for the purposes of the annual appropriation acts passed by Parliament following the budget.

The first set of output specifications was established in discussion between each department and the Treasury working with the State Services Commission and the Prime Minister's department. The central agencies provided advice and information to ensure the specifications were technically correct on performance measures and best practice. The nature of the exercise was to present in the new output format the activities that were currently being funded. As far as practicable, the Treasury sought to separate its role in this procedure from its traditional role of commenting on the worth of the expenditure on the outputs.

Not surprisingly, a great deal of debate ensued about the definitions of the outputs for each department. For the system to work as a whole, it was necessary that they be clear enough to enable the broader objectives of control to be met, while permitting much greater responsibility to be delegated to managers to find ways to deliver outputs within specified budgets and with incentives to manage efficiently.

Examples of outputs are shown in Table 2 illustrating outputs in the areas of policy advice, goods and services, the administration of regulations, and the administration of payments made by departments to third parties on behalf of the Government. Table 3 contains more examples.

The introduction of policy outputs in departmental performance agreements produced some controversy. The first consolidation showed that the Government spent about $NZ 343 million on policy advice in 1991/92, which seemed an astoundingly large amount. Under pressure from a select committee of Parliament, an investigation into the area was conducted by the State Services Commission (1991) to review the purchase of policy advice and identify options for improving cost effectiveness. The key recommendations that emerged were to establish a cap on expenditure on policy over the whole of Government and to make cuts over time, while setting priorities in a strategic planning and budgetary process. Performance information was to be developed, structural changes made to enhance

Table 2. Examples of Outputs

	Provider	Output: Title	Output: Description
Policy Advice	Police	Policy advice on policing property offenses	Policy advice on the effectiveness of police assistance to community support groups in reducing the incidence of property offenses.
Goods and Services	Department of Labour	Placement services	Provision of interviews with employers and job seekers, and referrals to vacancies and job clubs.
Administration of Regulations	Police	Licensing services	Administrative services for the issuing of licenses pursuant to the Arms Act and regulations.
Administration of Payments on Behalf of the Government	Ministry of Health	Health funding management	Negotiation, management, and monitoring of the Crown's funding of four purchasing agencies (Regional Health Authorities).

Table 3. Examples of Outputs from Purchase Agreements of Departments

Provider	Output: Title	Output: Description
Social Welfare	Policy advice on diversion	Policy advice on the role of social workers in the diversion of first offenders from the criminal justice system.
	Care and protection assessment services	This output involves the investigation of child abuse and assessment of the needs of children and young persons up to the age of 16 years, for care and protection.
Police	Custodial services	This output covers the provision of jailing services at police stations and courts for people under arrest or the subject of court orders. It includes the provision of escorting services to convey remand and sentenced prisoners to penal institutions.
	Vetting services	This output comprises the inspection of the records and premises of agencies issuing drivers' licenses pursuant to the Transport regulations.
Ministry of Defence	Policy advice on the EEZ (Exclusive Economic Zone)	Policy advice on the role of defense in the effective protection of the EEZ.

the focus of policy units, and coordination mechanisms to be developed to integrate policy across departments and to introduce quality management processes.

This centralized approach was not implemented, and instead, the Government sought improvements in policy advice within the decentralized management framework by directing the chief executives to attend to the issues. While the initial concerns had been over the total amount spent, the investigation revealed that much expenditure had been classified as policy analysis that was better described as ministerial servicing and communication and information services. These were reclassified in those terms. Also, ministers were persuaded that the budget for policy advice requirements in any area should be decided against competing claims within a department and reviewed within the budget process alongside other expenditures.

The inquiry spawned further initiatives to improve the effectiveness and efficiency of policy advice through quality management processes and policy coordination. For budgetary and management purposes, a distinction was drawn between policy research, which is an input to a department's primary functions (and therefore within the discretion of its managers) and that which is a final output being purchased by the Government and potentially able to be put out to competitive suppliers as a ministerial decision. For further information, see Claudia Scott (1992) and Hawke (1993).

The level of detail in the outputs varies for different purposes between departments. A department with many different outputs will list them separately, whereas some departments produce large volumes of homogeneous services and require less detailed specification. As an example, the Treasury has about 150 outputs, most of which are relatively small areas of policy advice of particular interest to the Minister of Finance, whereas the expenditure on the management of New Zealand's overseas debt is expressed in aggregated data.

In the agreements between ministers and their chief executives, there is more detail than emerges in the budget discussions between officials and ministers. The Appropriation Act presented to Parliament further aggregates the outputs. For example, the Treasury has nine outputs for which funds are appropriated.

The Public Finance Act permits the Government freedom to shift resources between the aggregate classes of output in Box 2, but only up to a tolerance of 5 percent. The Government must go back to the Parliament in a supplementary appropriation if it wishes to make larger changes, and in this way Parliament is far better informed about the purposes of the Government's financial plans and of significant changes in them. Within a class of outputs, the minister has the discretion to shift resources during the year, but is expected to consult the Cabinet if major changes are proposed to the plans that were presented to the Cabinet expenditure committee at the time of the budget. In well-run departments, there is regular reporting to the minister on variances from budget for the costs of the detailed outputs in the management plans with reports on how the excesses and shortfalls in funding are being balanced and requests for approval for changes in the scheduling of outputs.

On occasion, managers sought to weaken their accountability by arguing for very general output definitions that provided little outside information about the costs of the services they were providing. The first such attempt by the Customs Department, for example, included all its activities under one general output.

Outputs should make sense in terms of the internal management systems of the providers, although, in cases of conflict, it is the management systems that should be adapted to suit the outputs and not the reverse. As an example, the Department of Internal Affairs, which is responsible for numerous activities that have very little in common, organized itself around its regional offices and considered designating its outputs as the provisions and costs of those offices. This would not have given the Government information about the costs and performance of the individual programs; therefore the idea was dropped.

Across the whole Government, the implementation of the changes to management systems needed to meet the requirements of the two acts took eighteen months, and raised difficult issues, both conceptual and practical. For example, it was relatively easy for small policy advisory groups to reorganize their data on resource use into costings of the various lines of policy advice; they could use systems similar to those used by private sector consulting firms. By contrast, it was very difficult in the military because of both the nature of the output as a kind of insurance and some particular features of its production in New Zealand. These issues and the approach that was adopted toward defense outputs are discussed in Appendix IV.

Box 2. Treasury Output Classes

- Policy advice: general economic and financial strategies
- Policy advice: taxation
- Policy advice: demand and supply of goods, services, labor, and capital
- Financial performance of the Crown, and its departments, companies, and agencies
- Management of asset sales
- Budget management
- Crown financial reporting
- Actuarial
- Liabilities management

During the early years of implementation, the level of detail in the output specifications varied considerably from department to department. For some, it was a detailed description of services to be delivered, which also served as an internal management document. Other departments took longer to adapt to output-based management, and the output descriptors were general and not tied to internal management systems. In a few cases, this still applies today in the less well-managed organizations.

By 1992, the dissatisfaction expressed by ministers and the Officials Expenditure Committee with the excessively general descriptions previously involved in finance and budgeting led to the development of the concept of the *purchase agreement*. This provides more detail of service delivery commitments, especially for those departments that had provided fewer details of outputs in their performance agreements. The purchase agreement is used by the central agencies and ministers for budgeting and monitoring purposes. While the information in it is available for scrutiny by the select committees of Parliament, the Appropriation Acts still operate at the more aggregated classes of outputs.

The list below shows the structure of a purchase agreement and is taken from the table of contents from the purchase agreement for the New Zealand Defence Force.

Summary of outputs purchased
Parties to the agreement
Purpose and scope
Powers and obligations
Terms of agreement
Procedures for amendment
Monitoring and reporting
Interpretation
Payment

Rewards and sanctions
Dispute resolution
Signed statement

The outputs themselves are contingent military capabilities with specified levels and readiness, as can be seen from the example in Appendix IV.

Practical Approaches to Establishing Outcomes

The reason for the focus on outputs rather than outcomes was that outputs are a more objective basis for accountability relationships and more effective management: delivery of services can be more directly attributed to chief executives than can any ultimate consequences (outcomes) of that service delivery. If outcomes could be established with equal clarity and controllability by managers, then outcomes would be superior to outputs for specifying performance, as the risk of distorted incentives is reduced. In practice, there is a trade-off between the precision in performance specification necessary to get the efficiencies of a decentralized management system and the risk of distortion from poorly chosen outputs that are not effective in reaching the desired outcomes. Adherents to outcome-driven systems are focused on these potential distortions and emphasize performance indicators measuring outcomes.

The implications of this trade-off for a system that empowers managers to achieve specified objectives is that the objectives must be specified with care to ensure that they are contributing to the outcomes that are sought. This is not easy, although any outcome indicators that would be useful in an outcome-focused management system could be used, in conjunction with policy analysis, to check the alignment of the outputs with the relevant outcomes.

Superficially, the distinction between outputs and outcomes is simple and permits a useful role clarification between politicians and the professional managers required by a modern civil service. Implementation of this distinction can, however, raise very complex issues in some areas. There are limits to the extent to which the respective roles can be isolated from one another, except where the purchase relationship has reached the point of open competition between suppliers with no preferences for the public sector providers. Such cases are not durable anyway as privatization is the next step, there being no reason for government ownership to ensure the quality of services. In normal circumstances, the Government owns the public sector provider because it believes it is not possible or desirable to purchase the service in the open market. In this case, politicians will ultimately be concerned with aspects of management that raise political issues, and civil servants will ultimately be affected to a degree by the success or otherwise of their ministers. In New Zealand's experience, however, there is much to be gained in efficiency and effectiveness, by emphasizing the separation within these ultimate limits.

This not only is a useful principle for improved management, but also reflects the practical reality that, while some ministers may not like being publicly committed to outcomes by specifying them in writing, they are accountable for them whether they like it or not via the electoral process, crude as the feedback may be. A minister is expected by the public to be accountable for what his or her department is aiming to achieve, even if in default that is only what the department advised that minister.

It can also be seen as a benefit in a philosophical sense that the system of public sector management creates pressure to tilt the focus of the undertakings of politicians a little more in the direction of the consequences of government action rather than promises about managerial issues. For example, the public is ultimately better served not by a promise that "we will not privatize government's telephone company" but rather "we will ensure low prices and high levels of telephone service." The former is a much easier promise to fulfill, but what was the outcome being promised—"We will own the phone company for you"?

Boxes 3 and 4 illustrate some examples of outcome statements used in the system and recorded in the documents accompanying the Appropriations Act.

A simple distinction between outputs and outcomes might be thought to imply that there is, or ought to be, an outcome for every output. In fact, it is rarely possible to establish clear and unequivocal linkages between the outcomes that politicians seek and the outputs they require public servants to produce. Almost all outcomes are influenced by many different factors, and the provision of outputs cannot uniquely be associated with particular outcomes. By the same token, any output is likely to influence a number of outcomes, some of them perhaps in unintended ways. There are always side effects to any intervention that raise goal conflicts and force trade-offs.

As a typical example, in Singapore there is a government agency with the mission to encourage free traffic flow, which is effected in part by heavily taxing and prohibiting traffic. It is accepted that this could be adding costs to business and conflicting with economic development goals. In formal economic planning models, this is handled by assigning policy instruments to targets on the basis of their

Box 3. New Zealand Defence Force National Security Outcomes

- The maintenance of New Zealand's sovereign integrity and the development of its national profile.
- The promotion of New Zealand's exclusive national interests.
- The stability of the area of New Zealand's direct strategic interest (specifically Australia, South East Asia, and the South Pacific).
- The ongoing promotion of world peace and international stability.

Source: *Estimates of Appropriations of the Government of New Zealand for the year ended 30 June 1995.* Vote Defence Force, p. 236.

comparative advantage in affecting outcomes, in order to maximize the effectiveness of the policy mix and minimize unwanted side effects. In practice this is very difficult to accomplish. An obvious example is the assignment of the monetary policy instrument to controlling the price level in most countries.

In addition to accounting for side effects in mapping outputs into outcomes, there are huge gaps in information in most areas due to missing policy analysis and topics where such analysis is extremely difficult to conduct, regardless of the effort put into it. It is not possible to have a grand design in which all the links between the outputs of a government and the outcomes it seeks are mapped. All that is possible is groping for better outcomes through constant evaluation, adjustment, reprioritization, and redesign of outputs. Over time, the use of evolutionary processes of policy analysis and evaluation to design outputs, in the hope of achieving outcomes and to assess whether the expected results emerged, builds up knowledge of significant features of the output-outcome map. But the whole map is never seen at once, and it lacks a purely objective reality because it changes with the perspective of the viewer.

As a practical matter, governments deal with this intractable complexity by adopting various a priori principles, setting major strategic goals focused on a limited selection of outcomes, directing resources at what are thought to be the relevant outputs, and ameliorating the undesirable side effects that emerge.

The impossibility of mapping all outputs into outcomes and vice versa, while seeing all the goal conflicts and trade-offs, does not, however, prohibit the Government from specifying clear outputs it wants civil servants to produce any more than the impossibility of knowing all the options for personal mobility and their implication prohibits the purchase of a motor car. The question is about how much information and certainty is needed to make decisions that turn out to be correct most of the time. The output-outcome distinction is useful, by comparison with the traditional system, in clarifying the information that people in different roles need to do their jobs better while also strengthening their incentives to perform.

Box 4. Ministry of Agriculture and Fisheries Outcomes

- Benefit to all New Zealanders from the resources of agriculture being used in the most productive and sustainable way.
- An agricultural industry that is confident, self-reliant, profitable, and forward looking.
- Improved market access for New Zealand agricultural products. Increased export earnings from high-quality, innovative, and diverse agricultural products and services.
- A legislative and policy framework for the agricultural industry and rural communities that allows initiative, provides consistency and certainty, and ensures accountability.
- Maintained an improvement of New Zealand's plant and animal health status.
- Enhancement of New Zealand's reputation as a country largely free of plant and animal pests and diseases.
- New Zealand food products accepted as wholesome and safe to eat.
- Adequate access to information and basic services for rural communities.

Source: *Estimates of Appropriations of the Government of New Zealand for the year ended 30 June 1995.* Vote Ministry of Agriculture, p. 37.

The distinction has focused the attention of both supporters and critics of the system on the possibilities that well-produced outputs are producing undesirable outcomes, or at least outcomes that conflict with each other, thereby neutralizing their effects. However, this problem is not unique to output-based systems. The standard techniques of strategic planning, modeling, evaluation, and policy analysis can be applied to reduce that risk. The management incentives in the system may mean that more attention needs to be paid to the question than in a traditional system where efficiency in service production is not given such emphasis.

A recent example that illustrates this point lies in the administration of a policy of the Department of Social Welfare for recovering overpaid benefits and amounts that are owed to parents by their absent spouses but are paid to the parents by the department in the first instance. The management had established targets for each office around the country for the amounts to be collected, and was posting information about the performance of the offices in relation to the targets inside the department. Critics said that this had established a competition between the offices to collect the money, which was leading them to be too vigorous and not sufficiently sensitive about the circumstances of the people from whom they were collecting the money.

If centering managers' goals on outputs generates concern about potentially low outcome achievement, a management system focused on outcomes may be preferable. The consequences of such a focus for financial management would be for it to budget for and account for the costs of achieving outcomes rather than quantify the costs of production of outputs. That is the intention of the 1993 Government Performance and Results Act in the United States.

Weighing against the conceptual attractions of this approach are some practical issues. Outcomes are typically harder to define than outputs. The United States appears to be dealing with this issue in some of its early attempts to install results-based management by applying the designation "outcome" or "result" to variables that would be termed outputs in the New Zealand system.

An outcome-based management system is likely to dilute the accountability of managers producing outputs, as these managers have no control over many of the influences that can affect an outcome. A simple example of this argument is to measure highway road death statistics as an outcome of various related outputs such as road design, highway policing either in cars or with speed cameras, and publicity campaigns against drinking and driving. The policy analysis that links each of these outputs to the outcome and might gauge their relative effectiveness is not conceptually difficult. But there are many areas of public policy where the linkages are not nearly as clear and the effects can easily be swamped by other influences; for example, trade promotion activities could have their effects neutralized by movements in exchange rates or protection policies in foreign markets. Even the simpler example of the road death outcome could be greatly affected by petrol shortages or unusual weather conditions. Holding a person or institution accountable for an outcome cannot work if those responsible do not have control over the major instruments that affect that outcome.

A further consequence of the extra complexity of centering management on outcomes is the challenge of allocating costs to outcomes. For example, a decision might have to be reached on the proportion of highway construction costs to be allocated to the outcomes of economic development on the one hand and to safety on the other.

In an outcome-based system, therefore, the gains from targeting ultimate results are bought at the expense of lack of clarity in the specification and assessment of performance. The New Zealand system opts for greater clarity in performance specification, although this is intended to emphasize, and not to downplay, the importance of policy analysis and evaluation. It is worth noting, however, that New Zealand has not used program evaluation in the extensive way seen at times in Canada, Australia, and the United States.

Whatever may be the most effective blending of attention to outputs and outcomes in the long term, the practical problem faced in New Zealand was to decide the first step away from an input-based system. New Zealand sought the benefits of making departments expose what they produced with the resources they consumed. This new information base was influential in its own right in its effect on management decision making and budgeting. It exposed weaknesses in systems, structures, and the quality of management, and assisted the Government of the time to identify and prune back low-quality expenditures in some areas. There is no evidence that a systematic increase in emphasis on good management caused a loss of effectiveness in the contribution made by government policies to the achievement of the associated outcomes.

What is obviously important in any system of public management is that managers and staff should always be motivated to be concerned about the outcomes of their activities and strive for greater effectiveness in those terms. Output-based management need not conflict with this orientation and the wider managerial frameworks should ensure that they do not.

Contracting for Output Performance

Quality of service becomes a central issue when focusing on outputs. The traditional input-based system of management is unclear about the specific quality of the resulting outputs, although there are often implicit expectations. For example, the way in which staff in a social welfare agency deal with beneficiaries at the counter when they apply for benefits is a matter of concern to politicians, but their expectations in this regard are typically expressed in an ad hoc manner when a problem comes to their attention, or when they receive requests for extra resources to improve service. In an input-based system it is generally left to departmental managers to provide what they regard as a reasonable service, but only within their very limited freedom to manage resources. They will be restricted as to whom they employ, the wages they pay, where they locate, the premises they occupy, the layout of the premises, and other such considerations. Their scope for efficiently adapting their service to local conditions and to the expectations of clients is severely limited. Such a system will, however, produce a service that may generally be seen to meet community expectations, or, at least, to be all that the Government is willing to pay for. Typically, staff in the field have no alternative other than to refer complaints to their head office, which will, in turn, say it cannot do better without more resources.

Moving to an output-based system with deep delegation of managerial discretion frees managers to optimize the use of their resources in their local situations within the general central policy framework. However, the way in which managers choose to deploy resources can have major implications for the volume and quality of service delivered. Greater care may be required in specifying the underlying principles and objectives for the service as a whole, and in ensuring that these are understood by local managers. The search for efficiency can otherwise result in reduced service and in distortion of the Government's policies.

A well-specified output is described in terms of all the characteristics that are important to the Government for it to be assured of desired results, and important to the provider in designing and operating a production process that achieves those results efficiently. In practice, the generic characteristics of well-specified outputs are being discovered over time in New Zealand, through successive refinements in the annual budget cycle and, in some cases, through special reviews of some departments.

Where outputs are defined clearly there is greater potential for rapid improvement in efficiency and effectiveness, as managers are more aware of the results they have to deliver. They are also certain of their areas of discretion in decision making without concern over raising political problems for ministers by not delivering on expectations that were unspecified in their performance agreements, but were expected nonetheless.

As an example, the Income Support Agency of the Department of Social Welfare, which processes applications for welfare payments, is now clearly focused on assessing people's eligibility for benefits and issuing the checks (Box 5). With its clearly defined outputs and more effective management, it has cut the time for processing applications from three weeks to two days, and expects to reduce the time further to one day. It has also lowered unit costs. The local offices have been redesigned and the approach to dealing with the public and the community changed to provide a more effective service.

It is possible to argue, however, that if the outputs of this agency were badly defined in relation to the desired outcome and quality standards, staff might be encouraged to register ineligible individuals through not checking information adequately, or to save money by providing poor customer service and not drawing from the local community. Successful output delivery would not, in such circumstances, produce a satisfactory outcome. The example raised in the previous section relating to the collection of benefit overpayments by the same department is also relevant to this point.

The solution to the potential problem of distortion arising from the focus on outputs is partly to be found in clear specification of the nature and quality of outputs. Such specification may address service delivery, or it may identify client satisfaction goals, as would apply to the example above. Output quality is sometimes inherently part of the output definition, and sometimes is a qualifying commitment about the nature of the output and how and when it is delivered. It may be difficult to specify quality comprehensively, but a useful approximation may contain details about how the service is produced and monitored: for example, the quality commitments attaching to tax policy advice from the Treasury mention external review of major pieces of advice by experts.

The outputs were refined over time by the development of specifications for performance in terms of quantity, quality, and cost. The purposes of performance specification follow from explanations in

Box 5. Department of Social Welfare, New Zealand Income Support Service Outputs

- The provision of assessment services of applications for both primary and supplementary benefits payable under the Disabled Persons Community Welfare Act 1975 and the Social Security Act 1964, and applications for the community services card.
- The provision of review services for both primary and supplementary benefits payable under the Disabled Persons Community Welfare Act 1975 and the Social Security Act 1964.
- The provision of payment for both primary and supplementary benefits and grants made under the Disabled Persons Community Welfare Act 1975 and the Social Security Act 1964, and the issue of the community services card.
- The provision of activities to reduce the level of benefit crime, including deterrence investigation and the application of sanctions.
- The provision of activities related to the management of debts arising from benefits and pensions, and the collection of maintenance monies and liable parent contributions.

Source: *Estimates of Appropriations of the Government of New Zealand for the year ended 30 June 1995.* Vote Social Welfare, p. 897.

previous sections, and also emerge in Section VIII in the review of personnel issues. In short, performance specification and evaluation is used to

- demonstrate public accountability for output delivery through external reports of departmental performance;
- assist government decisions on the allocation of resources to policy priorities;
- assist in evaluation of the performance of departments and their chief executives;
- revise management control systems in the light of performance; and
- revise policy to attain greater effectiveness and value for money.

For these purposes, the various dimensions of the outputs must be measurable as far as practicable, but, in any circumstance, it must be possible to make an informed judgment about performance at the end of the reporting period.

Output Quantity

Table 4 contains an example of the specification of output quantity.

Determining the exact quantity of outputs is difficult where the factors that influence demand are outside the control of managers, so the ability to forecast output becomes important. New outputs for which there is no previous experience or for which policy is changing also add uncertainty. The new management regime created strong incentives for managers to forecast expenditures in order to control them; managers were thus required to stay within their budgets, and were given the means to do so. As a result, departmental forecasts of expenditures on outputs improved in accuracy.

Some services are, by nature, a contingency or a capacity to provide a service in circumstances that cannot be predicted. In New Zealand's agricultural economy, providing for the consequences of floods and droughts is an example. In these circumstances the performance specification includes a range of estimates as shown, for example, in Table 4.

The quantity specifications for policy advice are framed in terms of a work program of projects or routine responsibilities for which delivery can be established, as can be seen in the example in Table 4.

Output Quality

The quality specifications of outputs relate closely to the nature of the outputs in question. Quality specifications often have a major effect on the cost of an output, but, in line with private sector experience, there are possibilities for simultaneously raising quality and reducing cost. Redeploying underemployed labor and applying information technology are common instances. In New Zealand's experience, cost savings were, in many instances, redirected to improve service quality. Potential cost savings from applying advanced information technology to the Treasury's budget were continually absorbed by more elaborate budget documentation and by shorter intervals between ministerial budget meetings.

Quality stipulations focused on the requirements of clients, as determined either in consultation with them or with ministers as their agents, are obviously more legitimate than standards set by the providers themselves. Ministers have an important role in establishing the elements of quality in politically sensitive areas of service delivery. In other areas, the concern for quality is expressed in a more general way, with the specifics left to line managers who can take account of specific dimensions of quality in addition to the general concerns for accuracy, completeness, timeliness, and compliance with legal standards. Table 4 contains an example of quality specifications.

Output Costs

Production of outputs within agreed costs is a key performance measure. The costs for each output should be fully allocated by cost accounting procedures that reflect the true underlying consumption of resources. Unit costs can be measured wherever it is practical to establish measurable units of output, with large potential benefits for benchmarking costs and prices between similar public sector providers and enabling valid comparisons between costs in the public sector and the prices of similar services in the private sector. New Zealand has not adopted a formal contracting-out policy, but unit costing can create strong pressures on departments and ministers to keep costs in line with valid comparators, and to buy rather than make services where alternative suppliers have lower prices. The cost dimension of typical outputs can be seen in the example in Boxes 6 and 7.

Transparency and competition can also assist with the problem of incentives when poor quality flows from poor output specifications. In a setting where ministers and others have full information about the specific services being supplied by a department, and their cost, and they have some authority to acquire services elsewhere, the incentives exist to ensure that departments do not adopt a short-term, mechanistic approach to output production. Where a department has an active minister, or one who employs outside advisers to establish output specifications, there are incentives for managers to ensure that output specifications are clear.

Table 4. Examples of Output Quantity and Quality

	Provider	Title	Output Description	Quantity	Quality
Output Quantity	Ministry of Transport	Licensing of marine transport operators	Provision of a system of quality assurance on marine transport operators by means of entry control.	Marine certificates 1,000 Marine examinations 2,000 License applications 350 Applicants assisted 4,800 Issue of renewal of licenses 400	
Contingency Services	Department of Social Welfare	Assessment of disability grants	Assessing entitlement to a grant against predetermined criteria, determining the size of the grant and reviewing entitlement after six months.	Estimated at 2,400 assessments with a range of 1,600–3,200 based on 1993 data with 95 percent level of confidence. There will be a change in the cost of delivering this output if the number of assessments increases or decreases by 200.	
Output Quantity Specifications	State Services Commission	Policy advice on strategic human resource development	Policy advice on the most effective forms of strategic human resource development for the public service and the wider state sector.	Report on the performance pay survey by July 31, 1994; report on the development of promotion strategies for women in the public service by December 20, 1994; and review of senior manager training policies of three departments by October 13, 1994.	
Output Quality Specifications	Police	Custodial services	Provision of jailing services at police stations and course for people under arrest or the subject of court orders. It includes the provision of escorting services to convey remand and sentenced prisoners to penal institutions.		Ensure there are fewer than one (1) sustained custodial incident per 100 custodials. Ensure summonses are served in accordance with legal requirements with fewer than 1 percent sustainable complaints. Ensure all (100 percent) arrest warrants executed are in accordance with legal requirements.

Box 6. Cost Dimension of Typical Outputs

Provider:	Police
Output title:	Custodial services
Output description:	Provision of jailing services at police stations and courts for people under arrest or the subject of court orders. It includes the provision of escorting services to convey remand and sentenced prisoners to penal institutions.
Cost:	This output to be produced within the budgeted cost of $NZ 15,503,000.

Source: Example modeled after Purchase Agreement between the Minister of Police and the Commissioner of Police (CEO).

The solution is also to be found in the nature of the agreement between the departmental head and the minister. Performance agreements are between two parties normally committed to a long-term working relationship even though, constitutionally, one party is acting at the discretion of the other. Public servants are employed by the State Services Commission to serve the minister of the day, and carry a wider responsibility to the public service, Parliament, and the public to use their best judgment to act in the public interest. Therefore the public servant's incentives are to provide a high-quality service over time and to anticipate problems that might arise for the Government if any lack of precision in specification of outputs or quality were exploited to cut costs in the short term. If the public servant failed to act in this way, it would be regarded as a poor excuse to claim that the problem lay with the minister's lack of clarity in specifying what was required. This is not a situation that can be described by the aphorism "let the buyer beware" in a one-off purchase; it is an agreement between people with a mutual concern for a successful working relationship lasting over several years that will be damaged for both parties if poor services are produced.

Further, although there is normally no competition for the contract to do the work in the short term, in the longer term, poor performance will result either in dismissal or in the work shifting to another government department or to the private sector. Hence there is no incentive for the public servant to exploit the situation for some short-term gain at the expense of the longer-term performance and reputation of the department.

Promoting innovation in the delivery of public services requires care in defining service requirements in ways that do not fix irrevocably either the traditional services or the ways of producing them. Experience showed that people involved in day-to-day service delivery were likely to be a major source of new ideas about how to perform more efficiently and more economically; but they will be inhibited if output descriptions are too prescriptive or backward looking. New Zealand experience shows this is largely a matter of common sense, and the key is to focus on what is to be delivered rather than how.

Box 7. Wider Cost Dimension of Typical Outputs

Provider:	The Treasury	
Output title:	Policy advice: taxation	
Output description:	Provision of advice on tax policy, including advice on international taxation, personal taxation, indirect taxes, business taxation, tax systems, and compliance.	
Cost:	International tax	$NZ 1,286,000
	Personal tax	$NZ 562,000
	Indirect tax	$NZ 201,000
	Business tax	$NZ 2,171,000
	Tax systems	$NZ 468,000
	Ministerial servicing	$NZ 271,000

Source: Example modeled after Purchase Agreement between the Minister of Finance and the Secretary to the Treasury.

VIII Human Resource Issues

Senior Management

In designing the total system of reforms, the Government believed that the quality of the top management team was essential for achieving results. At the starting point in 1988, it was realized that the new requirements of managers would demand new approaches to their recruitment, remuneration, training, and development. While a few senior managers—the top three ranks in the departments—did not make the transition to the new system in that year, and a larger number were made redundant in the following years, the general expectation was that improved management would come in most cases from raising the skills of the people already employed in the public service. In many areas, it was not feasible to introduce professional managers who did not have the professional background and experience for the particular requirements of the departments. Persuading experienced managers in the private sector to join the Government was never going to be easy. In addition, much of the unsatisfactory management was attributed to the old systems and structures. On the other hand, it was realized that some individuals in senior positions would not succeed as managers and that the major organizational change required in a number of departments would need new officials in the top positions. The experience of the state-owned enterprise reforms supported these views.

The new systems for setting objectives, assessing performance, allocating resources, delegating responsibilities, providing incentives, and reporting on financial results created a floor below which performance could not fall—or made it clear as soon as performance dropped—because they ensured clarity in what was required and whether it was accomplished. The New Zealand system was not, however, intended merely to be management by objectives augmented by decentralization; such systems inevitably gravitate toward maintaining the status quo and focus on meeting minimum standards. To promote constant improvement in service and cost, departments must be continually searching for better ways to function and perform at levels above the targets set in the performance agreements. The bonus system for senior executives is therefore geared to reward performance above expectations.

If public services are to rise above the basic stipulations in performance contracts, it is essential to recruit and develop senior managers who have the technical skills and personal attributes to inculcate values of integrity and excellence and lead the departments to superior levels of performance. New Zealand's experience shows that the presence of top managers with these abilities is critical to the transformation of a government department. The performance management framework can show where performance is below or above specification, but cannot turn ordinary managers into great managers and transformational leaders. They must be recruited, or trained and developed.

The new procedure for appointing chief executives requires the chief commissioner of the State Services Commission to consult with the Government and particularly with the minister to whom the appointee will be accountable. The minister also has influence on the appointment panel, which is assembled for each appointment, and advises the commissioner on the best candidate. Typically, the panels will include prominent individuals in the community who are knowledgeable about the business of the department in question, and/or members of groups in the society significantly affected by the department's activities. The commissioner does, however, have the major say in which of the candidates is best suited for the job.

The commissioner then makes a recommendation to the Government, which normally accepts the recommendation, but is free to substitute another appointee if it chooses. In dozens of appointments since the new appointments procedure was introduced in 1988, the substitution procedure has yet to be used. On one occasion a recommendation was rejected without a substitute being appointed by the Government. The system does, however, permit a clear expression of the views of ministers to be provided to the chief commissioner, although it is not common for ministers to express strong views about candidates. There are no formal barriers to entry, and all jobs are open to applicants from the public and private sectors, including candidates who are not New Zealand citizens. The Director-General of Health appointed in 1992, for example, was a Canadian. There are no rights of appeal against appointments, although the Labour Court in New Zealand, which oversees industrial relations law, could hear a case on an appointment where procedures were alleged to have violated principles of administrative or labor laws.

Chief executives' tenure is for a maximum five-year term with no automatic right of renewal, although those who have performed satisfactorily are typically offered an extension for a further three years or encouraged to apply for a position as the head of another government department. The contract provides for dismissal for unsatisfactory performance. There is also recognition of the possibility of a fundamental incompatibility between the chief executive and the relevant minister that is not due to poor performance by the chief executive. In this eventuality the incumbent is either shifted to another position by agreement, or the contract is paid out. To the author's knowledge this provision has been used only once or twice. The exercise of these provisions would also be subject to appeal to the Labour Court, on grounds of either faults in the procedure or violation of the terms of contract. The procedure for performance assessment is described below in the subsection on incentives.

Remuneration is determined provisionally by comparison with the salaries of similar jobs in the private sector, as assessed by standard international systems of job sizing and pay research. These systems typically analyze a job in terms of skill levels, responsibilities, and the amount of risk being carried. In this way, it is possible to attain comparability between jobs that are not necessarily similar in terms of the business in which the manager is employed, but are similar in terms of the factors that determine remuneration levels within private sector corporate structures (Boxes 8 and 9).

New Zealand salaries were struck at these levels of comparability with the private sector as senior civil servants moved from permanent tenure to five-year terms. This process involved substantial pay increases for those in jobs with heavy responsibilities. The highest salary set was that of the chief executive of the Treasury for whom a total remuneration, including actuarially estimated pension benefits and a car, amounted to approximately $NZ 215,000—about US$100,000, at the exchange rate at that time. Officials in smaller departments without heavy responsibilities did not receive much extra over their existing salaries and they expressed their dissatisfaction with the methodology that was used. The point at issue was whether officials in control of small but influential policy departments carried positions of greater significance than allowed for under standard pay methodologies.

Box 8. Salaries for Heads of Departments/Branches of the State Services, December 1, 1986

Salary	Position or department
$NZ 83,325	Government computing Government printing Tourism and publicity Valuation Women's affairs
$NZ 96,250	Conservation Customs Environment Forestry Government life Housing Internal affairs Lands and survey Maori affairs Prime Minister Public trust Rural banking and finance Survey and land information Statistics
$NZ 101,750	Agriculture and fisheries Defence Forest service Inland revenue Labour Parliamentary counsel office Social welfare State insurance Trade and industry Transport
$NZ 107,250	Crown law Education Energy Foreign affairs Health Justice Scientific and industrial research Works and development
$NZ 115,500	Post office Railways Treasury

Source: *Higher Salaries Commission General Review*, December 1, 1986.

Box 9. Public Service Chief Executives' Remuneration, June 30, 1994

Salary band	Position or department
$NZ 80,000 and below	Ministry of Youth Affairs
$NZ 80,001–90,000	Ministry of Cultural Affairs Ministry of Pacific Island Affairs Ministry of Women's Affairs
$NZ 90,001–100,000	National Library Department Parliamentary Services
$NZ 100,001–110,000	*Clerk of the House of Representatives Customs Department Education Review Office Ministry of Forestry Ministry of Housing Ministry of Maori Development (Te Puni Kokiri) Department of Statistics
$NZ 110,001–120,000	Department of Conservation Government Superannuation Fund Department Department of Internal Affairs Department of Survey and Land Information Ministry of Transport Valuation Department
$NZ 120,001–130,000	Ministry of Education Ministry for the Environment Public Trust Office *Deputy State Services Commissioner
$NZ 130,001–140,000	Ministry of Commerce Ministry of Defence Department of the Prime Minister and Cabinet Ministry of Research, Science, and Technology Serious Fraud Office
$NZ 140,001–150,000	Ministry of Agriculture and Fisheries *Chief Parliamentary Counsel Department of Labour
$NZ 150,001–160,000	*Controller and Auditor-General Ministry of Foreign Affairs and Trade Inland Revenue Department Department of Social Welfare *Solicitor-General
$NZ 160,001–170,000	*Chief of Defence Force Ministry of Health Department of Justice *State Services Commissioner Treasury

*Remuneration determined by the Higher Salaries Commission.

Source: *State Services Commission Annual Report for the year ended 30 June 1993.*

Because New Zealand was going through a period of difficult economic adjustment, the salary levels of chief executives drifted steadily away from their private sector benchmarks, after being set at those levels in 1988, in exchange for ending permanent tenure, and now are as much as 30–50 percent below them. This has caused some dissatisfaction, but appears to be having little effect so far in terms of retention of individuals in top jobs. The downstream effects on recruitment are hard to gauge, but are likely to be serious. The chief commissioner has formally stated that this situation is a major concern to him. The politicians currently in power, however, have not felt inclined to face the opprobrium that accompanies paying large salary increases to public servants. In 1995, after three years of economic growth, some increases were awarded.

The new appointments procedure was intended to develop as wide a recruitment pool as possible for senior civil servants in order to promote innovation and fresh thinking about issues and policy, service delivery, and management, and to introduce a wider set of perspectives from the community as a whole. This is unlikely to happen if all the appointments are of officials who have spent all, or most, of their careers working their way up the civil service hierarchy. Even with market-based remuneration, however, it has not been easy to recruit individuals from outside the Government who are better prospects than the internal candidates. Surveys showed that managers in the private sector often regarded working for the public service with disfavor. They saw the service as lacking a supportive performance climate, and disliked the "fishbowl" environment in which executives, especially those in high-profile departments, had to work. Good private sector candidates need to be sought out by skilled executive search firms that keep in touch with the careers of competent managers in the public and private sectors.

Private sector culture typically provides for an appointment process that is more certain and rapid than in the public sector, where the procedure described above can take a long time and may also involve a person's candidacy becoming known. Private sector managers seeking top jobs also typically expect a greater degree of authority over their actions than the public sector can offer. The systems of parliamentary accountability, the rights of ministers to direct, and of Parliament to publicly scrutinize activities, are usually negative features of the jobs from a private sector person's viewpoint.

There remains a significant difference in culture between the public and private sectors, although the new regime has closed that gap substantially and in desirable ways. Even with this new regime and the high visibility of, and general public support for, the reforms, appointments from the private sector into the senior civil service in New Zealand have been few and far between. A retired chief executive of a major New Zealand company did, however, serve as head of the Ministry of Defence. While a certain proportion of outside appointments is a healthy sign, it should generally be expected that top-quality internal appointees present themselves as candidates for top jobs.

The basic requirements for a chief executive in the public sector are a mixture of special attributes specific to the public service, and others similar to those of a chief executive in the private sector. The task includes managing the external environment of the organization; strategic planning, with a longer-term focus than that of the line managers; managing external relations with key people and with organizations whose interests intersect with those of the department and the ministers it serves; and managing relationships with the minister and the Government more widely. A chief executive must also develop, represent, and constantly reinforce the values and culture that underlie all the organization's systems, objectives, and day-to-day activities.

Finally, the post of public sector chief executive requires all-round leadership closely resembling that which the private sector encourages in its thinking about the leadership responsibilities of chief executives. Of the large number of managers in the public service, only a handful have the capability and motivation to deliver high performance required of a chief executive. The pressure for change today is far greater than in former times, and this is reflected in far greater demands on senior public servants' technical abilities, management skills, and leadership qualities. This pool of talent does not accumulate naturally and needs to be nurtured and developed. A center for strategic resource management has been established in New Zealand that is controlled by the group of chief executives themselves in partnership with the State Services Commission, using techniques adapted from advanced private sector practice. Studies have been performed to identify the competences that characterize the top-performing chief executives. Some of these are generic to all senior managers and others are specific to the nature of the particular task.

From the information on chief executive competences, it is intended that individual training and development programs will be assembled for every person in the pool of potential senior management talent, after they have been assessed against the demonstrated standards. The development programs will entail some standard management training courses, but will heavily emphasize on-the-job training and development to gain day-to-day experience in areas where competence is to be enhanced. The programs are also likely to incorporate gaining experience in different departments and in the private sector, or in other countries. To ensure that individuals in the potential senior management pool have the opportunity to benefit from individual development programs, the programs will be entered into the personal employment agreement between the employee and his or her chief executive and then monitored by the State Services Commission.

The State Sector Act provided for the establishment of a Senior Executive Service (SES) that encompasses the pool of managers at senior levels and acts as a focus for the wider collegial interactions of members, with an emphasis on training. In fact, the SES was only a partial success and was not supported by many senior managers who saw it as constraining salary movements and providing inferior training activities.

Industrial Relations

New Zealand has a long tradition of industrial relations laws, customs, and institutions that, until the 1980s, emphasized tripartism between the central organizations of the trade unions, employers, and the Government. Although the formal general wage adjustments across the economy had ended with the reforms to macroeconomic management during this period, the legal and political relations between the public sector unions and the Government were a significant feature of the environment in which the reforms took place.

As labor is the major cost in producing most public services, the system for delegating control of costs to managers who had been used to the previously centralized regime raised many industrial relations issues. Because the Government was dissatisfied with the performance of the public service and was looking for change, it sought to negotiate reforms with the public sector unions over an extended period. After some time, however, the Government concluded that changes that could be negotiated were insufficient for the achievement of the proposed reform goals, and implemented the reforms unilaterally. This led to resistance from the public sector unions.

Although chief executives were made the legal employing authorities of workers in their departments in place of the State Services Commission, the law required that, in exercising their rights as employers, chief executives were to be "good employers." In practical terms, this meant establishing personnel management systems that emphasized principles of equal opportunity, observance of the rights of New Zealand's indigenous Maori people, and processes that emphasized transparency, merit, and various rights of appeal or review of decisions.

The practical implementation of personnel management reform in each department was left to the interplay of management and employee interests, against the background of the introduction of performance requirements for chief executives and tight, usually shrinking, budgets. A major objective of the New Zealand reforms was flexibility at departmental level, in contrast with many other countries that have sought Government-wide policies on particular industrial relations issues, such as performance pay.

As a consequence of the changes, the system of occupational classes with detailed pay ladders, through which staff progressed on the basis of seniority, was replaced by a system of "ranges of rates" that could apply to a job; the particular rate was set by management on the basis of qualification and performance. Departmental managers could decide whether to introduce performance pay systems, and, in fact, many did not. Transitional issues proved to be very important. The previous system had established expectations of automatic progression up the remuneration ladder over time. The new "range of rates" approach established pay through benchmarking against wider pay research, with margins of up to 20 percent for performance pay. There was little resistance to the introduction of the "range of rates" approach, even though it put an end to entrenched expectations about annual wage increases. Large numbers of civil servants have had little or no increases as a result. A variety of pay systems have arisen, as thought appropriate by departmental managers. Some departments have paid targeted performance bonuses and given little or no general increases. Progression to higher pay levels is possible only on the basis of performance, except for the bottom one or two rates within the range. Typically, performance is reviewed annually, but pay increments are not automatic.

Under the previous system, a large number of occupational groups struck pay scales in separate negotiations. As a result of the changes, amalgamations have produced a much smaller number of groups, with a range of rates established for each.

Notwithstanding the decentralization of remuneration determination, the State Services Commission coordinates interdepartmental discussions on a consensus view of labor market conditions before negotiations with the unions begin. The Government may, from time to time, impose a limit on any overall general pay increase that is to be granted, and has over the past three years directed that there will be no compensation in the budget round for general movements in pay.

Union representation of public sector employees has generally been withdrawn from middle management, although this varies from department to department. Officials reporting to chief executives have their pay and conditions determined by individual negotiations with the chief executives, within the basic framework of a five-year contract subject to some oversight of remuneration levels by the State Services Commission. Chief executives are, however, free to negotiate individual contracts outside this framework with individuals at senior levels, but generally do so only where particularly specialized skills are needed.

While the general approach to human resource issues is decentralized and flexible, some measures of overall coordination and administrative guidance continue to circumscribe the authority of departmental managers. There is a strong consensus among chief executives that their ability to improve the performance of their departments is critically dependent on local autonomy, and they are vigorous in resisting any central encroachments on their managerial freedoms.

IX Decentralized Financial Management in Core Government Administration

This section describes the financial management regime that was put in place to support the wider philosophy and concepts of decentralized management in core government administration. A system was required that would support plans for delegating to managers considerable autonomy over all the resources needed to produce specified outputs, while also holding them accountable in detail for delivering the specified outputs on time and within budgeted costs. The system was further required to provide better information and incentives for ministers in allocating resources to changing priorities within the budget process, and lastly, to provide improved information to Parliament, the Auditor-General, and the public.

Financial management in government is conventionally defined as the processes of planning and programming; budgeting; budget execution and accounting; and audit and evaluation.

Issues in planning and evaluation comprise the relationships between outcomes and outputs in the New Zealand system, and involve policy analysis and review functions and analysis of the Government's interests from an ownership perspective. Section XII relates this approach to those found in other countries that place heavy emphasis on programming and evaluation systems. The discussion below is organized around the topics of budgeting, operational management (which is the approach to budget execution), accounting and financial reporting, and external review.

Public Finance Act

The Public Finance Act, 1989, and subsequent amendments, provides the legal framework that underpins all aspects of the financial management regime, together with the Fiscal Responsibility Act, which is described below. The main features of the Public Finance Act

- developed (1) the definition of performance in terms of outputs and outcomes, (2) the distinction between purchase and ownership interests, and (3) the distinction between the whole government accounting entity and the individual departments;
- removed many administrative controls;
- made chief executives responsible for departmental financial management;
- established departmental and Crown reporting requirements;
- provided for the use of generally accepted accounting principles, from which it followed that accrual accounting was required; and
- redefined the basis of appropriation from programs to outputs.

Under the broad provisions of the Public Finance Act, a financial system was developed that was designed to clarify the accountability of chief executives and to remove their responsibility for factors over which they had no control. Departmental balance sheets were separated from the Government's wider balance sheet. For example, the national parks are on the government balance sheet whereas the Department of Conservation, which manages them, has on its balance sheet only those assets necessary for that task, including improvements to the parks themselves. Following the same principle, payments going to government departments for the production of services were distinguished from payments passing through those departments, for example, welfare benefits as they are passed on to third parties.

Budgeting

Parliamentary Control of Supply

In New Zealand's constitutional arrangements, Parliament has traditionally appropriated cash to the executive to spend on inputs. The controller function was exercised by the Controller and Auditor-General, who authorized the release of money from the public account—essentially the Government's account at the central bank—on being satisfied that there was an appropriation against which the payment could be charged, and that the spending was for a lawful purpose. Authority to spend, or "supply," arises under Appropriation Acts or Imprest Supply Acts pending an Appropriation Act. There are established conventions governing how long the executive can continue with Imprest Supply Acts before bringing an Appropriation Bill to Parliament. As a formality, the Governor-General signs "warrants" that permit the executive to spend up to a specified amount on the advice of the Controller and Auditor-General. The warrants are initialed by the Secretary to the Treasury, whose staff monitor the Government's use of supply and advise the Government when a further Appropriation or Imprest Supply Act is needed.

Shifting to an accrual-based system undermined the significance of cash control, which either had to be abandoned or modified to suit the new approach. It could be argued that an ex ante control mechanism was no longer necessary with tighter specifications of the purposes of appropriation and reporting requirements. The Government decided otherwise. It was thought that the right to withhold cash was still needed as response to a situation where appropriations were being exceeded. To control supply on an accrual basis is difficult and ineffective. For example, assets would continue to depreciate and departments could obtain credit, so it is impossible for Parliament to block the executive's access to resources measured in an accrual accounting context.

It was decided to institute a system in which the legislature's control of the flow of cash going to the Government is retained, while, at the same time, the Appropriation Act is expressed in terms of total resource use. In effect, a breach of accrual appropriations is the trigger, while turning off the cash is the weapon. The control of cash acts as a proxy control that works indirectly, as it is likely that credit would dry up very quickly and other actions would be taken once it was known that the flow of cash had been cut off. The concept of cash control operates on a gross basis, covering all government expenditure regardless of offsetting revenue flows. The documentation accompanying Appropriation Acts is expressed in terms of the total resource costs of providing the outputs that have been contracted for by each minister.

The control is exercised on payments from the Crown bank account, which, in reality, is a suite of bank accounts including the settlement account at the Reserve Bank, the main Crown account at a private sector commercial bank (Westpac), subsidiary accounts at Westpac, and accounts at overseas banks operated by the New Zealand Debt Management Office (NZDMO). A daily controller statement is prepared by the Central Financial Controller's office in the Treasury, and contains the amounts it proposes to pay from the Crown bank account for (1) disbursements to the departmental bank accounts in accordance with agreed cash profiles; (2) payments by the NZDMO for investments or debt purposes; (3) and disbursements to subsidiary accounts operated by departments making payments to third parties on behalf of the Crown.

The controller statement is prepared two days in advance of the day on which the disbursements will be made. It is accompanied by a reconciliation of the accumulated cash disbursements with the supply available from accumulated warrants, known as the warrant availability reconciliation. The daily statement is reviewed by the Auditor-General, who certifies the statement after being satisfied that (1) the payments are covered by a warrant; (2) there is an appropriation against which the payment can be charged; and (3) the purpose of the expenditure is lawful.

The crucial question as to whether the Auditor-General can refuse to certify is best described in a quotation from a policy paper prepared by the Treasury (1989):

> The Audit Office may refuse to certify the statement in whole or part where it is not satisfied that the above conditions are met. Where the refusal relates to a particular department exceeding an appropriation, no disbursement to that department's departmental bank account can be made. Thus if a department exceeds a cost appropriation for one class of outputs and is likely to incur further costs (e.g., depreciation) all disbursements of cash to that department (for any purpose) can be stopped.[9]

The Auditor-General monitors the flow of accrual financial data from departments, but would advise that the cash supply be turned off if the expenditure were not in accordance with Parliament's authorizations. In keeping with the principles of the accrual-based appropriations, the cash flow to the departments is not specifically identified with individual appropriations. The implications for the monitoring of departments are that the Treasury monitors, through monthly departmental reporting, all expenditures in relation to each type of appropriation for each department or other agency. These reports are passed to the audit office. Where the report shows that a department is approaching the maximum amount of an appropriation, the Treasury warns the audit office so that it can monitor the expenditure carefully and investigate the department more closely if it wishes.

Appropriations

The financial management system has implications for the structure of Appropriation Acts.

[9]The Treasury, *Financial Management Policy Guideline Number 8. The Controller Function,* p. 3, November 1989.

Whereas it was previously common to vote resources to a department that serviced several ministers, this created internal conflicts over resource use. The solution was to identify with one minister only the resources voted for each purchase agreement between a minister and a department. It follows that a minister with more than one portfolio might be served by several departments and has no authority to shift resources between them. Where a department serves several ministers, it will receive several votes and the chief executive may have several purchase agreements although, more commonly, they are merged into one for fulfilling that component of that executive's performance agreement. Each department has a responsible minister, typically the minister with the largest purchase interest, who is concerned with the ownership interest in the department. If there were conflicts between multiple purchasing ministers, the responsible minister would reconcile the differences.

The accrual accounting concepts also changed the way in which appropriations for long-term investments are made. The Government, as owner of a government department, has an interest in encouraging managers to provide the contracted outputs efficiently, which means with as small an asset base—as represented in the balance sheet—as possible.

Managers have the freedom to optimize their asset base, which includes purchasing replacement assets by using funds generated by depreciation. For most departments, this involves a rolling replacement program, in which new assets are purchased using the cash set aside through the application of the depreciation formula in setting the costs of outputs for which the legislature provides the funds. Where a department must expand its asset base, the cost of new assets exceeds the funds being generated by depreciation; and a cash injection is then required that fills the gap between the total cost of investment in any year and the funds generated by depreciation. The documentation underlying the Appropriation Act, therefore, also provides for these capital injections.

The payments made by departments under entitlement programs, such as welfare benefits, or at the direction of government, are not part of the income and expense statement of a government department because managers are accountable only for managing the payment flows and not the flows themselves. These funds are appropriated separately from appropriations for outputs.

Where departments receive money from the sale of services or collection of fees from parties other than the Government, the appropriation by Parliament is on a net basis. This permits the department to spend money it has received from third parties. The resources coming from the Government for services it purchases are thereby linked with revenues from trading with third parties in the departments' underlying business plans, but costing and accounting conventions are used to ensure that trading activities are not covertly subsidized by funds that were intended for providing services to the Government. Where an asset is disposed of below book value, an appropriation for the shortfall might be required in unusual circumstances where the allocation of the cost to an output, which would normally occur, would lead to unacceptable pricing.

Types of Appropriation

The 1994 amendment to the Public Finance Act[10] established the types of appropriation available as follows:

- classes of outputs to be supplied by departments and purchased by the Crown from another person;
- benefits or other unrequited expenses;
- borrowing expenses;
- other expenses incurred by the department and the Crown;
- capital contributions comprising any increase in the Crown's net asset holding in the department, or capital investment by way of equity or loan in another person or organization;
- the purchase or development of capital assets by the Crown; and
- debt to be repaid by the Crown.

The concept underlying the appropriation for other expenses is that these costs cannot reasonably be passed onto purchasers of the services, usually in a commercial setting.

Appropriations are approved annually, but there is a multiyear forecasting basis for fiscal planning and budgeting. Each budget cycle begins on the basis of the forecasts made a year earlier for the year ahead. Multiyear appropriations are provided for in the Public Finance Act but have not been used so far, although they are under consideration as a future option. They do not legally bind a future Parliament, although they would create a certain degree of commitment that would be awkward to avoid. Instances have occurred where the executive has struck a deal with a department that gives the department assurances of the levels of funding that will be in the Appropriation bills in future years, although this does not legally bind Parliament at that time. The reforms brought about dramatic enhancements in the information accompanying the Appropriation Acts. The

[10]New Zealand Government, *Public Finance Amendment 1994* (Wellington), pp. 12-13.

Box 10. Environmental Hazards Control

Description

Subsidies are provided to regional councils for a combination of measures that reduce community risks from environmental and physical hazards. Control measures may include the implementation of a combination of economic instruments (e.g., compensation for conversion of mining right privileges) with physical remedial or preventive works. Physical measures may include flood protection works, erosion control in high-priority catchments, remedial works for environmentally degraded water bodies, and the cleanup of contaminated sites.

Outcomes

This output class will contribute to
- reduction of Government's liability as insurer;
- protection of communities against environmental and natural hazards; and
- maintenance of enhancement of the nation's international environmental reputation for trade and tourism.

Performance measures

Quantity and timelessness
- Construction of stop banks on the lower Waihou River completed by April 31, 1995.
- Cleanup initiated on the two highest-priority contaminated sites by June 30, 1995.
- First year of a five-year program of soil conservation planting for five high-priority catchments covering 3,000 hectares in Gisborne District completed by November 1, 1994.
- First year of a three-year program for the treatment of five high-priority environmentally degraded water bodies completed by June 30, 1995.
- Construction of one river control works initiated by June 30, 1995.

Quality
- Construction of Waihou Valley Scheme works in accordance with the advice of its Technical Advisory Committee.
- Cleanup of contaminated sites in accordance with recommended remedial measure.
- Remediation measures for environmentally degraded water bodies and land carried out in accordance with and under supervision of water quality scientists and soil conservators.

Cost

Outputs in this class will be provided for the appropriated sum of $NZ 4.702 million inclusive of goods and services tax.
- Significant providers.
- Regional councils, with Waikato Regional Council being the major provider with the construction of the Waihou Valley Scheme.

Source: *Estimates of Appropriation for the Government of New Zealand for the year ended 30 June 1994.*

estimates documents for the 1987/88 year included the following illustration, which was one of the two pages relating to the Ministry for the Environment.[11]

Ministry for the Environment
Program: Administration and General
To provide the Government with advice on matters relating to the physical and natural environment and to implement the Government's environmental policies. This also includes the cost of providing corporate and ministerial servicing (Box 10).

Compare the data in Table 5 with the information provided in the 1994/95 estimates for one of the nine classes of outputs alone.

Budget Processes

It was apparent from the beginning of the reforms that the most important impacts the Government could have on the serious fiscal situation were its decisions about expenditure levels and priorities. Fi-

[11]Ministry for the Environment, *Estimates of the Expenditure of the Government of New Zealand for the year ended 31 March 1988*, B.7, Pt. I, p. 81.

Table 5. Ministry for the Environment Appropriations
(In thousands of New Zealand dollars)

		1986/87	
	1987/88	Voted	Expended
Personnel	2,160	551	625
Operating costs	1,755	384	524
Capital	700	124	39
Grants	44	—	—
Transfers (goods and services tax)	462	84	60
Total	5,121	1,143	1,248

Source: *Estimates of the Expenditure of the Government of New Zealand for the year ended 31 March 1988.*

nancial management reform was merely a tool for better decision making but could not ensure improved fiscal policy. Government commitment to an orderly budget process was seen to have a major impact on the quality of the outcome. Experience in the United Kingdom in enforcing cabinet discipline on the budget process during the early years of the Government of Prime Minister Margaret Thatcher was influential. The Australian system of budgeting was seen as a model in terms of processes and documentation.

New Zealand's budgetary processes had previously demonstrated a tendency for consideration of the details of a budget to overwhelm the development of general agreements at the strategic level about the direction of fiscal policy. Experience also showed that even relatively minor misunderstandings about information protocols and timetables for forecasts and decision making were the cause of serious problems in the assembly of a budget and in the fiscal outcomes.

The major objective in the redesign of budgetary processes was to establish stable processes that would strengthen the influence of broad fiscal policy objectives, and set an envelope over the detailed expenditure and revenue decisions that emerged. In 1989, the Government attempted, but finally abandoned, an effort to make a major fiscal statement at the beginning of the budget cycle. The idea persisted, however, and gradually emerged, one element at a time. It is now a legislative requirement: as the Fiscal Responsibility Act passed by Parliament in 1994 requires the Government to make an annual statement of its fiscal views and plans in a budget policy statement and to publish detailed long-term projections of the fiscal situation. It also requires the Government to explain its fiscal policy at the time of the budget by reference to its prior fiscal policy commitments in a fiscal strategy report. These and other requirements are explained in the subsection below on parliamentary scrutiny. The point to be made here is that over many years, the budget process has been made increasingly predictable and stable. Orderly, logical processes and information requirements have finally been written into law. Appendix II shows the annual financial cycle of the Parliament.

Departmental purchase agreements are developed with ministers, with budgetary constraints in mind. They are then subject to detailed scrutiny by the Treasury and other central agencies, to test for consistency with the broad directions of government policy. The process looks to impose more detailed pressure on specific expenditure elements, taking account of views of the effectiveness of activities and the efficiency of management. In the jargon of the system, there is advice given about purchase and ownership interests. This information is submitted to a group of senior ministers who make up the cabinet expenditure committee and make recommendations that go to the Government as a whole for final decisions about the policy mix to be incorporated in the budget. As in any country—however intellectually rational—approaches to budgeting run up against political approaches emphasizing power, personalities, and coalitions. The view is widespread among the participants that the financial management framework has strengthened both the influence of rational elements in the debate and the macro-overview of fiscal policy.

New Zealand's experience has shown repeatedly that an orderly and strategically driven budget can be drafted only if the Minister of Finance has the authority to control and manage this process, and has the unequivocal backing of the Prime Minister. The rights of ministers to bypass the Minister of Finance and the cabinet expenditure committee to approach the Prime Minister directly have to be circumscribed. Observing Australian success in controlling expenditure in the 1980s by having the Prime Minister directly involved in the review committee reinforced this view.

The information systems supporting fiscal and financial management have been progressively developed to the point where they are now fully integrated in concepts and operations. The budget will, in future, be prepared using the same financial management information system that aggregates the financial performance of the departments and produces the financial statements of the Government. Accrual accounting, for example, is now the basis of the preparation of departmental resource bids and of the estimates presented to Parliament.

Operational Financial Management

Financial Delegation

All the input controls were removed and Treasury instructions withdrawn, to be replaced with new instructions governing accounting policies and the operational areas of financial management, covering reporting obligations, foreign exchange management, investment of trust funds, and the management of bank accounts and contingent liabilities. Appendix I contains the table of contents from the new Treasury instructions.

Departments were given freedom in the acquisition and mix of inputs, including staff and capital items. They now have the authority to buy and sell assets within the department's overall level of net capital, without appropriation. Virtually all provisions compelling chief executives to acquire such services as accommodation, vehicles, computers, and office services from central monopoly providers were removed. Chief executives were given the power to operate their own bank accounts and the authority to manage their cash.

The legal basis of the freedom to manage departmental finances stems from legislation that covers the rights of the Government to spend public money and to delegate this right to others. The Public Finance Act sets the basic constitutional rules, and the annual Appropriation Acts authorize the executive to expend specified resources allocated by output classes, with limited freedom to shift resources between classes. The executive may shift up to 5 percent of the funds authorized to an output class to any other output class without the approval of Parliament.

During the fiscal year, a Supplementary Appropriation Act may be passed to appropriate further resources, or it may shrink the resource availability where output requirements have been reduced or unexpected cost savings made. Ministers in charge of each portfolio are voted the right to spend the money by Parliament. They in turn delegate this right to the chief executive, who, under the law, is responsible for the financial management of the department. The department is responsible for administering the vote, and it has no right to borrow.

Only the Minister of Finance has the power to borrow on behalf of the Government. The Minister of Finance also has the power to issue guidelines about prudent financial management and instructions about high-risk financial transactions such as the investment of trust funds. Good practice guidelines have been issued for all major areas of financial management. In certain areas, policies must be negotiated between the Ministry of Finance and the department, covering areas of significant risk or technical complexity, for example, policies on insurance and on the management of foreign exchange risk.

Departments are now free to operate their own bank accounts, but the Government's interest in optimizing its management of financial assets and liabilities leads to restraints and incentives on cash management activities. The restraints and incentives are examined in the subsection below on debt and cash management.

Measuring Financial Performance

Performance is defined so as to distinguish between the Government's dual interests in the performance of a department: on the one hand, as the owner of the department seeking efficient use of its resources, and on the other hand, as the purchaser of the services being delivered by the department, either directly to the Government itself or to third parties. The purchaser is looking for a given quality of goods and services at the best price.

Distinguishing between these two perspectives lends greater clarity to the specification of performance expectations. Ultimately, the only reason the Government owns a department is to obtain services from it for itself and for third parties. If it thought the services could be obtained more cheaply and more effectively from the private sector, there would be no rational basis for having the department.

As the owner of the assets and liabilities of a department, the Government is concerned to have available a form of financial reporting that values the assets and liabilities that are under the control of the department's managers. This enables the Government to make a judgment about the effectiveness of resource management. The authorities chose a statement of financial position or balance sheet, broadly similar to that presented to the shareholders by the managers of a large private sector company, as the appropriate reporting format. Besides expenses incurred in the consumption of resources in the current year, the Government is interested in the consumption of assets that have been purchased in prior years. This is recorded in the same way that standard accounting practice requires, through the depreciation of assets over their lifetime. The money coming from the Government to fund the purchase of resources is entered in the income statement as revenue in the same way that revenue from sales is recorded in a private sector company.

By using these standard accounting documents in an environment of considerable management freedom, the Government can assess the effectiveness of management in minimizing the resources required to do the job. The balance sheet information, over time, enables management to be assessed on whether it has sold excess assets or redirected them to other purposes that are no longer needed, or are obsolete. The record of management in reducing current liabilities can be similarly assessed.

Output Cost Accounting

The Need for Accurate Costs

The Public Finance Act, 1989, placed a much greater emphasis on the role of costing in the appropriation process for government departments than was previously the case. Prior to its introduction, the cash basis for appropriations for the inputs required staff to have only basic budgeting and accounting skills in order to identify the various input costs incurred annually by the department (e.g., salaries, travel, accommodation, energy, and communications). Typically, this information was based on the previous year's expenditure reports, adjusted for any incremental changes in activity identified for the future year.

The introduction of appropriation by output, accompanied by a change from cash to accrual accounting, introduced a complex new set of arrangements for departments that were developing accounting systems for the first time as part of the introduction of decentralized management. The change to accrual accounting in itself introduced new challenges. It required departments to separate operating expenditure from capital investment and to identify new types of input costs, such as depreciation on fixed assets or consumption of inventory that had not been recorded under the cash accounting convention. But, most significantly, it required the department to identify the outputs that it produced and then to assign all of its costs to those outputs.

Output costing was a new and unfamiliar concept for many departments. Defining the departmental outputs in the first place was not always straightforward, and often required extensive debate between the department and the Treasury to agree on definitions. A common problem was to distinguish between an intermediate activity and a final output. For example, the flying hours provided by frontline Air Force aircraft on operational tasks were held to be a final output, but flying hours on the same aircraft for pilot conversion training would be regarded as intermediate activity, and, therefore, an input.

The costing procedures that flowed from the output definitions needed to reflect the rationale behind the definition. It became essential for departments to assign input costs accurately to outputs, since the output became the criterion by which the appropriation decision was made. Ministers had to make purchase decisions as to the mix and quantity of outputs to be delivered by departments in the forthcoming year. Failure by a department to assign its costs accurately to its outputs could lead to budgetary difficulty where the revenue earned from supplying outputs failed to cover the actual cost incurred in producing them.

Costing Principles

The principles underlying output costing in the public sector are similar to those employed in the private sector to cost products and services. A significant difference between the two sectors lies, however, in the way in which the cost information is used. In the private sector, product costs are used to assist with decision making and planning (e.g., to decide whether a product is profitable and to assess the level of sales that must be achieved to break even) but prices are usually set independently by market forces (except where "cost-plus" pricing agreements are in force). In the public sector, where the department is often the monopolistic supplier of the output, there is no market price, so the output costing methodology has been adapted to establish the purchase price for the purposes of parliamentary appropriation.

The basic principle of product costing is to identify all resources consumed directly in the production of the product, and to cost those resources. The greater the degree of direct costs that can be identified, the more robust the cost. Other resources that cannot be traced directly to the final product are treated as overhead costs and are usually allocated to products on an essentially arbitrary basis (e.g., corporate services costs are often allocated according to the direct labor cost of the product). Cost allocations reduce the utility of product costs as a basis for decision making, since they do not accurately represent the relationship between production volume and resource consumption.

The problem of cost allocation is greater in organizations where overheads such as corporate services and information technology represent a high proportion of total costs and are spread across multiple products. This is typically the case in government departments, particularly policy departments (service delivery departments usually have significant resources directly attributable to outputs). The fact that output costs contain a substantial allocated cost component creates problems for the department whenever the purchase decision is changed from the original budgeted level. While revenue received by the department will vary directly with quantity supplied, the costs incurred by the department will not necessarily vary in the same proportion due to the allocated component being unrelated to resource consumption. The recent introduction of activity-based costing (ABC) in costing techniques represented an effort to address this problem.

ABC is a costing approach that specifically addresses the problem of overhead cost allocation and links overhead resource consumption more directly with output levels. Although developed initially by private sector manufacturing organizations, it has been applied successfully to service organizations. As such, it provides a valuable tool for government departments in addressing output costing issues. ABC differs from traditional cost allocation by seeking to identify the cost driver for a particular category of overhead, rather than by simply applying an arbitrary allocation basis. Using ABC, organizations identify the factors that drive their overhead costs. In the service sector, for example, banks have found that their information technology (IT) costs for electronic banking are dependent on their customer profiles, with high-wealth individuals making infrequent but high-value transactions, while low-wealth individuals typically make frequent but small transactions that place greater demand on IT resources. IT overheads could, therefore, be allocated to banking services on a more meaningful basis using an ABC approach based on customer profile, instead of an arbitrary allocation basis.

Best Practice in Output Costing

Costing techniques employed by New Zealand government departments have varied according to the size, type, and complexity of the organization, and the sophistication of the costing system available to them. Some departments, such as Inland Revenue and the Treasury, use staff time sheeting systems to track the consumption of labor resources and to charge labor costs to outputs. Time sheets provide a useful tool for assigning direct costs to outputs, but the information gathered must still be interpreted carefully by decision makers. For example, the New Zealand police allocate direct labor and other costs to categories of incident on the basis of the length of police time recorded against it. In reality, the resources used for policing minor incidents are available only when there is a lull in high-priority activity.

This form of costing may give an incorrect impression that low-priority tasks have a cost similar to high-priority tasks, and may tempt decision makers to cut back on the expenses of responding to low-priority incidents. In fact, this would lead to a cutting back of resources needed to be on stand-by to respond to high-priority incidents. An ABC system might overcome this problem with time sheeting by identifying the high-priority tasks as cost drivers and allocating more of the cost to the high-priority incidents.

Other methods of assigning costs to outputs are also widely used by departments and include the following:

- *Activity review* is a form of standard costing that uses a sampling study to conduct an analysis of staff activity over a period of time. The analysis is then used to project total labor costs on the basis of the standard established in the sample study.
- *Resource accounting* attempts to measure each output's consumption of direct resources, using extensive internal metering and monitoring systems. For example, the operation of telephones, photocopiers, central processing unit time, and electricity can be measured and charged to specific users if suitable metering equipment is installed and internal procedures are implemented.
- *Output accounting* uses the general ledger in the accounting system to assign output codes to different categories of costs.
- *Management judgment* is sometimes used as a surrogate for a formal costing system. In the absence of a formal costing system, managers are required to use their experience to estimate each output's use of resources and to attribute costs on the basis of such estimates.
- *Cost center accounting* is a frequently used approach to output costing, where input costs are first collated by a cost center based on the organizational structure. Cost center costs are, in turn, assigned to outputs using a predetermined allocation formula.

Implementation Issues in Government Departments

The introduction of output costing in departments gave rise to a series of implementation issues that required resolution. Many departments did not have staff with cost accounting skills, and, as this need became apparent, considerable recruitment of staff from the private sector and the accounting profession took place. The sudden demand on this limited pool of available skills created shortages, and departments experienced some difficulty in recruiting suitably qualified personnel.

The shortfall in qualified departmental staff was offset to some extent by widespread use of consultants to assist with the selection and implementation of new financial management information systems and the design of cost allocation mechanisms. Many departments were setting up decentralized accounting systems for the first time, and lack of experience led to a number of problems. Some departments with large sunk investments in computer hardware chose accounting software that was specific to their particular platform but was not necessarily the most suitable solution for their organizational needs. A common problem was that departments bought systems that were more sophisticated than was required, with the result that they had greater difficulty in setting up and running their systems.

Challenge of Costing Defense Outputs

The definitions of outputs have major implications for the method and complexity of cost measurement, and caused some departments great difficulty during the implementation phase. The New Zealand Defence Force presented difficult challenges in this regard. The treatment of defense outputs is described in some detail below to illustrate some of the complexity of defining and costing outputs. The approach described brought huge gains in information quantity and usefulness, although the concepts are still open to debate.

Outputs were centrally defined in terms of their various elements—that is, ships, aircraft, and army units. These terms described the various Defence Force elements in terms of what they are rather than what they do. The elements proved relatively easy to cost, as they were effectively categories of input, but they failed to describe the services that the Defence Force provided. Subsequently, the Defence Force redefined its outputs in terms of the contingent military capabilities and annually provided services (e.g., search and rescue operations) that the Defence Force provides to the Government. A contingent military capability is defined as "equipment and manpower maintained and trained to a level, set against specified preparedness conditions, from which an operationally effective force element can be generated when required,"[12] for example, contingent military capability to conduct antisubmarine operations. While this makes more sense to Defence Force managers in terms of output planning, and to politicians in making choices and funding decisions, it proved much more complicated in terms of costing.

A defense capability is a combination of numerous factors. Moreover, a major unit such as a warship can provide a number of capabilities simultaneously. The problem of joint product costs thus emerged, a situation familiar to accountants in process industries such as oil refining. The Defence Force initially took the approach of allocating these joint costs evenly across the various capability outputs, since there is no "right" or "wrong" method of allocation in this instance. However, the cost information was of little use from a decision-making standpoint. The Defence Force has continued to revise its approach to output costing, and is currently looking at forms of activity-based costing to provide more meaningful cost data.

The size and dimensions of a military capability are manpower and its state of training, and equipment and its condition. These are tightly interwoven. Some cost elements can only be varied over long time periods whereas others can be raised or lowered in the short term. The fixed capital costs of equipment are the major part of the funding requirement for most outputs. The effectiveness of a military capability is related to preparedness, which depends on readiness, deployability, sustainability, and combat viability. Some of these factors affect the capability as a whole and some affect particular components.

Each defense force element can be kept at a different level of capability, from a minimum level to an operational level, with a specified degree of notice required to reach the latter. A force element is defined as "the smallest size of readily identifiable, discrete units which can if required operate independently and which comprise an operational force."[13]

The activities that translate inputs into output capabilities are (1) enabling activities to support defense force elements; (2) readiness training activities; (3) sustainability activities that support a deployed force at its operational level of capability; (4) overhead activities; (5) and annually produced service activities.

Readiness training activities have the main effect on their operational level of a capability and on the annually produced services. Such activities are the main link between resources and capabilities—that is, inputs and outputs. Readiness training is further broken down into core competency training (e.g., safety drills for weapons training) and task-specific readiness training (e.g., firing for frigate crews).

For each defense force element, the readiness training and associated costs established are those necessary to maintain an operational level of capability. The associated costs of sustaining that level over the estimated time of operation are also assessed. In addition, the specified level of preparedness below the operational level, and the degree of notice and viability period, are taken into account and the training activities necessary to maintain that preparedness are specified and costed. Activities are separated into those that are specific to the military tasks of the output group and those that are common to all outputs to which the defense force element contributes. A high proportion of costs fall into this latter category.

Costs are first budgeted at the cost-center level to reach a total input budget, which is then assigned to outputs through the activities and associated outputs. Activity costs are grouped into the five cate-

[12] New Zealand Defence Force, *Estimates of Appropriations of the Government of New Zealand for the year ended 30 June 1995*, pp. 227–70.

[13] New Zealand Defence Force, *Estimates of Appropriations of the Government of New Zealand for the year ended 30 June 1995*, p. 236.

gories noted above. The task-specific portion of readiness training and the annually produced services are allocated directly to outputs. Overheads supporting the defense force collectively are allocated to capabilities, and the remaining indirect costs are allocated to Defence Force elements as set out in Table 6.

The costs of defense force elements are attributed to outputs on the basis of activity measures such as steaming days for ships.

It is accepted that the approach to costs allocation illustrated in Table 6 resulted in greatly improved information for assessing the purposes of defense outputs and the resources used, although there remains some debate over the process of appropriating for contingent military capabilities. Critics argue that allocating the costs of force elements to contingencies lacks a solid basis, as the total cost of owning and operating a force element could be allocated to one of many possible contingencies depending on which one becomes a reality. The force elements are in effect insurance against multiple contingencies.

Current Situation

By 1994, all New Zealand departments had a minimum of three years' experience in operating output costing systems. Some of the initial problems, caused by lack of skills or inadequate information systems, were ironed out, and output costing has become a routine part of the appropriation and management process. However, departments continue to refine their costing methodology, and to develop output cost information to improve resource allocation and service delivery.

An example of an area of continuing adjustment is the Department of Labor, which undertook an ABC exercise on a major output category (Placement Services) that places the unemployed in jobs. It used an ABC approach to identify the IT and other resources used in the provision of the placement output. During this exercise, the department discovered that client type was an important cost driver for some resources. For instance, more staff time was consumed in trying to place more highly educated applicants into suitable job vacancies than applicants with average educational levels. Other client variables such as ethnicity and geographical location were also shown to exert a significant impact on costs.

The implications of the influence of client profile on service delivery, resource usage, and costs have not been explored or developed by most New Zealand departments. For departments that interact directly with the public, there is considerable scope to improve costing systems through addressing the impact of their client profile on their cost structures.

Some Lessons from Experience

The following are some lessons from New Zealand departments' experience in operating output costing systems.

• Careful definition of outputs is a critical factor for both departments and the Government. The utility of both output cost information and performance measurements hinges on the proper definition of the departmental outputs.

• Departments must acquire sufficient expertise in costing and financial management to function effectively under the output appropriation regime. It is likely that new financial and costing systems will need to be introduced into departments, and there will be a period of increased workload and a steep learning curve for staff.

• Full costing of outputs depends on an accrual accounting regime being introduced in place of the traditional cash accounting regime. Retention of

Table 6. Defence Force Costs Allocation

Costs Associated with	Allocated to	Based on
Enabling activities	Units supported by the activity	Resource usage
Overhead activities	Force elements	Personnel numbers
Core competency activities	Force elements	Force element that undertakes the activity

Source: New Zealand Defence Force.

cash accounting would mean that many production costs would not be reflected in the output cost.

• There is good scope for modern cost accounting techniques such as ABC to be introduced into departments, with effective results. Departmental managers obtain a better understanding of their cost structure, while Parliament can make a more rational decision on the level of appropriation to be approved.

• It has taken time for output cost information to become useful to decision makers. This reflects both the initial difficulty in correctly defining departmental outputs and in developing adequate costing systems.

Debt and Cash Management

The financial management system led to changes in the concept of cash management by government departments. Under the previous system, the Treasury's bank account with the central bank was used as a checking account on which were drawn payments to third parties. The Treasury issued checks on receipt of authorizations for payment from the spending departments. In later years, the central system became overloaded leading to greater delegation to departments to issue their own checks.

Under the new system, the departments issue checks from their own bank accounts. Through a competitive tendering process involving all the major commercial banks, a contract was let to the Westpac Banking Corporation to provide commercial banking services to all the government departments. This contract comes up for renewal periodically and covers the conditions under which basic banking services will be provided and charged for. A large discount below normal commercial rates was obtained through this centrally negotiated contract. Departmental requirements for services other than basic banking services are left to the departments to arrange for themselves. Requirements differ substantially, and this arrangement enables each department to purchase the services it wants, such as foreign exchange services or credit card services. The new system yielded considerable improvements over the previous arrangement, which forced all departments to take the banking services offered by the central bank, although these services were inferior to the private sector alternatives. It made no sense for the Government to invest in the infrastructure to provide better services from the central bank. The advantages of scale and technical specialization in risk management are retained through centralized management of the Government's aggregate cash position.

At this stage of the technological development of New Zealand financial markets, it is not practicable to allow government departments to choose any commercial bank they wish, while still satisfying the objective of central management of cash. At some point in the future, such an option is possible.

The Treasury's NZDMO branch was established to assume the responsibility for managing both the Government's cash position and its portfolio of domestic and foreign debt. The Government's short-term debt management, using Treasury bills, is managed through a contract with the Reserve Bank of New Zealand, which is New Zealand's central bank. The NZDMO is organized in both structure and function in a way that is very similar to a typical corporate treasury in a large corporation with many subsidiaries. There is a research group, a portfolio strategy function, a small dealer team, a back office settlements team, and a cash management group.

Departments are responsible for managing their own cash in accordance with an agreed plan at the start of the financial year after discussions with the Treasury, and as an element of the budget preparation. The profile of cash balances in the department's bank accounts on a monthly basis is forecast for the year, taking into account all the planned inflows and outflows from expenses, revenues from parties other than the Government, asset and liability management, and the resource consumption approved in the Appropriation Act. The approved resource consumption is named "Revenue Crown" to emphasize that it represents a payment for services to an entity whose accounts include an income statement and a statement of financial position.

As the year progresses, the cash flow forecasts are constantly updated and fine-tuned. The releases of cash into the departmental bank accounts are timed differently for separate departments, reflecting the nature of the businesses. The cash implications of capital spending are that departments with approvals for investments in excess of their depreciation flow will receive cash injections for the difference. Running down the level of investment below depreciation has the opposite effect. The lumpiness of investments can also lead to accumulations of cash. It is a matter of government decision whether the buildup of cash in these circumstances is invested somewhere awaiting a drawdown to finance an investment, or whether the Government chooses to finance the investment from taxation or borrowing when payment is due, and then make the cash injection at that time.

Departments are subject to interest rate rewards and penalties as an incentive for effective management of working capital (current assets and liabilities). Penalty interest rates apply on loans to departments that run out of cash, whereas interest is paid on surplus funds. The highest rate paid, however, is on balances that are in accordance with the previously agreed plan. This rate is close to, but below, the rate for short-term money in the money markets.

The further the actual balance departs from the plan, the less is paid. The NZDMO will pay a market rate for term deposits from departments for money that is to be set aside for a period of time.

The effect is to reward managers for keeping to the profile of cash requirements that was negotiated with the Treasury at the start of the year. The logic is that every business has an optimal level of cash that negotiations should seek to establish, and the incentive system should be geared to encourage adherence to the cash profile.

Besides administering the incentive system for departmental cash management, the NZDMO sweeps departments' bank accounts each evening and invests surplus cash in the overnight money market. This innovation generated savings—by comparison with departments' previously idle balances—of about $NZ 30 million a year.

Planning for the management of the Government's debt begins each year at the time of the budget. The NZDMO prepares for the Minister of Finance's approval a borrowing program with the details of how the Government proposes to fund the net cash deficit for the year. Note that this is the traditional cash deficit and not the accrual-based fiscal deficit measure that is at the center of the economic policy debate. This borrowing program includes the profile of cash releases into the departments' bank accounts, the forecast of receipts from taxation and other sources, forecasts of other government expenditure, and the servicing of existing debt.

The NZDMO's objective is to minimize the net cost of servicing the Government's debt obligations over time, within the constraints of a portfolio management objective to minimize risk from the variability of interest and exchange rates and from liquidity and credit risk.

Charging for Capital

A symptom of weakness in the previous financial management system had been the accumulation of assets that had not been intensively used. The authorities encountered difficulty in securing information on all the assets owned by departments, even though the Government had on several occasions directed that asset registers be completed. The requirement that generally accepted accounting principles be adopted resolved this problem as audited statements of financial position were required, but an incentive was needed to encourage effective use of assets.

A charge for the use of capital was introduced from July 1991. In a manner analogous to the payment of dividends on a shareholder's funds in the private sector, an interest rate is charged to each department annually. The amount is determined by applying an interest rate to the net worth figure in the departmental statement of financial position. The underlying philosophy was to establish a cost basis for government activities that promoted clear information for comparative purposes within the Government, and between the Government and the private sector. It was intended to assist in establishing cost benchmarks both for monitoring the efficiency of management and also as an input to decisions regarding the contracting out of services. It follows that the interest rate should in principle be the cost of capital for similar activities in the private sector, on average. This can be calculated by the conventional capital asset pricing model. As this raises practical difficulties in many areas of the Government (e.g., establishing the appropriate beta coefficient for the diplomatic service) a default rate was decided on that was used in cases where the theoretically correct method could not be applied.

The amount of the charge was set at 13 percent for two years, and was then reduced to 10.8 percent as interest rates in the private sector fell. Conceptually, this rate is the taxpayer's opportunity cost of capital, adjusted for the same class of risk. The rate is, however, established as a default rate whereas the underlying concept is that the rate charged to any department should be pegged at a level equivalent to the weighted average cost of capital for similar activities in the private sector. A number of departments have negotiated particular rates with the Treasury. These rates have not turned out to be higher than the default rate generally because the latter rate had an upward adjustment built in to take account of the fact that the Government's borrowing costs were lower than the private sector's because of the access to the taxpayer to back the credit risk.

Results of Implementation

The capital charge has raised the general level of awareness of the implications of investment in assets and working capital for the cost structures of government departments. Departments incorporate capital expenditure programming into their planning and have formal processes for evaluating capital expenditure proposals. New Zealand no longer has a centrally administered hurdle rate for reviewing all public investment proposals, although very large items are subject to Treasury scrutiny and decisions by the Cabinet.

An independent review conducted in mid-1993 endorsed the regime, but showed variation in the extent to which government departments had implemented detailed internal capital charging, although it is uniformly included into costs in any area where fees are charged to third parties. As more sophisticated product-costing systems are introduced for departmental outputs, the capital charge will be translated into cost

Box 11. Management Framework Surrounding a Chief Executive

- Employment contract for five years with a possible extension based on performance.
- Possibility of receiving performance bonuses for performance above expectations, or of being criticized or dismissed for performance below expectations.
- Commitments in the performance agreement regarding strategic results, key result areas, outputs, and management or ownership issues.
- Forecast financial statements and other accountability documents to be provided by Parliament.
- Personal responsibility for departmental finance.
- Annual report to Parliament on performance of department based on standard questionnaire by the Finance and Expenditure Committee.
- Audited statement of service performance.
- Freedom to manage staff without central regulations.
- A fixed amount of resources on an accrual basis, either net or gross, depending on the potential for earning third-party revenues.
- Budget based on resources for output production.
- Monthly monitoring of financial information by the Treasury.
- A degree of competitive pressure from alternative suppliers, depending on the outputs whose costs are measured in the same way.
- A charge similar to a dividend for capital invested in the department.
- Interest rewards and penalties for variations in cash balances from agreed levels.
- Freedom to manage balance sheet within these constraints but need for Parliament's approval to expand the capital base.

estimates more widely. Some departments have introduced internal systems for charging rents for the use of land, buildings, and vehicles; the rents incorporate the capital charge of one business unit in a department that supplies these facilities to others.

The responsibility for managing the capital charge, particularly in departments with very large asset bases, is typically delegated from the chief executive officer to an individual with responsibility for managing major assets. The regime has made departmental financial managers aware of the methods of financial analysis appropriate to assessing the cost of capital, and, in particular, the capital asset pricing model. The awareness of financial risks in government activities has also been heightened.

In some cases, the incentive effect was initially undermined because people saw it as a bookkeeping transaction and did not see the potential for more effective management of assets and liabilities. The fact that the Government did not guarantee that it would not extract excess funds once these were released through better management of assets was seen by some departments as undermining their incentives, although others saw it as the means to meet savings targets imposed on them while not cutting back on plans for improved service delivery. A considerable and continuing effort in communications has been necessary to ensure wider understanding of these concepts.

At the time of introduction of this scheme, departments were provided with the extra funds needed to pay the charge. Subsequently, it had the effect of encouraging departments to use assets more productively, dispose of assets that were no longer needed, and manage debtors, creditors, and inventories more effectively. This was especially effective at times when budgets were being cut and increased services demanded. Departments found ways to maintain service levels with smaller asset bases.

Management Framework Surrounding a Chief Executive

Box 11 provides a summary of the main features of the management environment surrounding the chief executive of a central government department.

Earlier in the reforms, the departmental corporate plans were seen as part of the accountability documentation for Parliament, but, in the light of experience, a distinction has been drawn between the two. The information needed for the purposes of appropriation has been separated from departmental reporting. Corporate plans have begun to diversify from standard formats according to departmental views about the audiences for these documents. Whereas the Ministry of Commerce puts out a corporate plan of a high standard but in a traditional format, the Ministry for the Environment, which has extensive responsibilities for communication with a wide variety of community groups, has moved to different types of documentation altogether in aiming at these groups.

The incentive system was designed with an emphasis on performance, and the key to evaluating

Box 12. External Reporting of Departments

The annual financial statements of departments include the following items:

- statement of financial position;
- operating statement;
- statement of cash flows;
- statement of objectives;
- statement of service performance;
- statement of outstanding commitments;
- statement of contingent liabilities;
- statement of any unappropriated expenditure; and
- statement of accounting policies.

Source: Ministry of Agriculture and Fisheries, *Annual Report*, June 1994.

the accountability framework is to consider its effects on the chief executive, who holds the performance levers. The external framework has the details listed above but in essence it poses five questions to a chief executive. At a broad level of generality, strategic result areas answer the question "How does your organization's mission contribute to the Government's wider goals?" Key result areas answer the question "What is important for you to achieve within this year's operational requirements in order to contribute to the Government's wider goals?" The outputs concern the purchase interest question "What are you actually producing now and are they worth what the Government is paying for them?" The outcomes concern "What are the consequences of your outputs on the community in terms of government policy objectives?" The ownership analysis, which examines business plans extending into the future, asks both "Are you getting a satisfactory rate of return on the resources invested in your organization?" and "Where do you expect your organization to be in a few years and how are you positioning it for the future?" These issues overlap and apply at different levels of generality but collectively constitute the main questions faced by managers in this performance management framework.

Accounting and Financial Reporting

Setting Accounting Standards

Good accounting practice emphasizes materiality and relevance, and derives from underlying principles of good stewardship. Professional financial managers make judgments based on these principles, and do not adopt mechanistic formulations. Where, for example, a business is sufficiently simple that a cash accounting system is an adequate representation of its affairs, then there is little point in going to more complex systems. For any significant activity in the public sector, however, it is appropriate to use full accrual accounting methodologies to provide timely and accurate reporting.

The objective of accrual accounting is to ensure that the accounts for any one period of time accurately represent the total resource flows in the period. The accounts should not be distorted by differences from year to year in the outstanding debtors, creditors, unusual payments, and receipts from asset acquisition and disposal—thus avoiding distortions in the picture of underlying resource usage that cash accounts can produce.

Accrual accounting also captures information faster than cash accounting by taking account of commitments for the future that have been entered into, but for which no payment has occurred. The application of generally accepted accounting principles, therefore, leads to the adoption of full accrual accounting; this follows in turn from the requirement for information about the ownership interest the Government has in a department.

The generally accepted accounting principles used in New Zealand by professional accountants in the private sector are now employed in the Government, as a requirement of the Public Finance Act. This ensures that standard accounting conventions are used throughout the Government, and enables valid comparisons to be made between government departments and equivalent private sector activities in order to better assess performance (Boxes 12 and 13). The accounting profession, represented by the New Zealand Society of Accountants, issues statements to its members about proper accounting practice. These standards are now mandatory in the private sector as a result of the Financial Reporting Act, 1994. The national professional body is also linked to international conventions that are constantly being updated by international and national accounting standard setting groups.

Box 13. Government Financial Statements

The financial statements of the Government consist of the elements for departments in Box 12, without the statement of objectives, but with the following:

- statement of responsibility;
- statement of borrowings;
- statement of unappropriated expenses;
- statement of emergency expenditure or expenses;
- statement of trust money;
- notes to the financial statements; and
- report of the audit office.

These are accrual-based statements for the whole government entity.

Source: *Financial Statements of the Government of New Zealand for the year ended 30 June 1995*, pp. 32, 33, 37, 44–47, 60–70, and 77–109.

Generally Accepted Accounting Practice

The Treasury states in its guidelines to departments that

> The term generally accepted accounting practice (GAAP) is defined in the Public Finance Act to mean:
>
> - Approved financial reporting standards (within the meaning of Section 2 of the Financial Reporting Act 1993) so far as those standards apply to the Crown or the department or the Office of Parliament or the Crown entity;
> - In relation to matters for which no provision is made in approved financial reporting standards and which are not subject to any applicable rule of law, accounting policies that are appropriate in relation to the Crown, departments, offices of Parliament or Crown entity and have authoritative support within the accounting profession in New Zealand.[14]

In practice, the adoption of these standards enabled the entire accounting systems of the Government to be revised and upgraded over two or three years. The upgrading was relatively rapid because the standards and conventions already existed and the accounting profession, as either consultants or recruits into the public sector, could build the new system much more quickly than would have been possible if specialist public sector accounting expertise had been required. While this may appear to have run the risk of bringing inappropriate accounting conventions into the public sector, this turned out not to be the case.

As for most countries, the generally accepted principles in New Zealand allow other countries' conventions, when they are seen to be relevant, to be adopted where there is no national standard. Public sector accounting standards are generally not as highly developed as private sector standards, and there is also considerable variation from country to country. Many of the conventions used internationally have been developed in the United States, Canada, and other countries.

An important question was whether to establish specialized public sector standards or to aim at uniform accounting standards to be applied in both the public and private sectors. Whereas some countries have decided on specialized public sector standards, the approach that is being adopted in New Zealand is to have similar conventions in both sectors, except where specialized issues arise. The generally accepted accounting principles explicitly allow for the substitution of accounting conventions when these have to be specifically tailored to the requirements of a certain situation in order to replace more general conventions. Further, the areas of greatest contention about the applicability of private sector accounting conventions in the public sector turned out not to be very important in terms of the objectives of the total financial management system. In particular, issues about the valuation of "community assets" are irrelevant to establishing the financial performance of government departments because these assets are contained in the Government's balance sheet and not in those of the departments themselves. These valuations did, however, affect the Government's consolidated balance sheet, but they only add an extra question to be settled in interpreting the meaning of a government balance sheet as opposed to the interpretation of a balance sheet in the private sector.

Generally, accounting professions the world over are dominated by private sector accountants who have not paid much attention to public sector accounting standards. It is, however, common for the accounting profession to have a public sector body within it. In New Zealand's case, the senior public sector financial accountants became prominent in the Society of Accountants and, in particular, the public sector group within it. Their work in generating accounting standards reached a point where they were breaking new ground on issues that were also relevant for the private sector. As a result, the accounting profession has agreed to a single set of standards for both sectors. A spin-off benefit of this cooperation is that the public sector can contribute to the development of higher standards of accounting practice. Some interesting issues in the application of the generally accepted accounting principles had

[14]The Treasury, "Accounting Policy Parameters," *Treasury Instructions* (Wellington), Section II, p. 6, 1995.

to be resolved; for example, the methods of valuation of assets and liabilities.

The NZDMO regularly "marks to market" the portfolio of government liabilities in order to capture the real economic information in current market prices and values necessary for management and reporting. Private sector financial assets and liabilities are also commonly valued this way for management purposes, although they are typically reported at historic cost in financial statements, reflecting the internationally accepted practice. Within the general convention to value on historical costs, New Zealand private sector standards are more inclined than other countries to use the flexibility available to revalue assets and liabilities to reflect market values in terms of what is known as "modified historic cost." The public sector conventions push this flexibility further to get closer to the real economic values used in public policy analysis.

The public sector financial statements lean more to current values than general practice, while staying within the general principles. Putting the current market values of the debt into the government financial statements would have meant departing from the generally accepted accounting principles on a major issue at that time. It was decided that the market valuation should be provided as notes to the accounts, while the historic values of the debt were recorded in the balance sheet. As current cost data are used in assessing the performance of the portfolio managers, and are widely used in private sector financial institutions, these data need to be reported. The view was taken that the use of historical cost conventions is justified on the grounds that constant revaluation of assets and liabilities is impractical and undesirable. The reason for the use of the convention is that it is well understood, easily audited, permits comparability between accounting entities, and allows adjustment to or interpretation of the data from a familiar starting point.

The question arose of how to consolidate state-owned enterprises that are 100 percent owned by the Government. The private sector convention rests on ownership and normally requires full consolidation when a subsidiary is 100 percent owned, because there is complete control. The State-Owned Enterprises Act, however, establishes a self-denying requirement on Parliament to stay out of management decision making. It is also an important part of state-owned enterprise policy that the entities do not carry a government guarantee, so that the managers are forced to satisfy their debt holders about the prudence of their management. The Government had no intention of running its enterprises as if they were subsidiaries of a holding company; its intention was to be a passive shareholder insofar as business strategy and decision making was concerned. In view of these unique aspects of the situation, it was resolved that the modified equity method of consolidation was the appropriate technique. This approach was preferred by the Finance and Expenditure Committee of Parliament, which is a primary audience for the accounts.

Accrual Accounting as a Management Tool

The question is sometimes asked whether the introduction of accrual accounting justifies the costs. New Zealand's experience suggests that costs are not particularly large and that the benefits in terms of improved external reporting are considerable, but the major benefit in terms of contributing to improved performance comes from its use in a decentralized financial management system. It is a necessity in this context to limit the total resources available to managers largely free from central controls. Once Finance and Expenditure Committee accrual accounting is in place, it becomes possible to create strong incentives and pressures for efficiency through better management of balance sheets.

The Government can fix the price it is prepared to pay for outputs while managers shift resources to best advantage and release funds from underutilized resources. This can be seen in the following quotations from the minutes of a Cabinet meeting in 1994 that addressed requests for capital contribution:

- "A capital contribution from the Crown is the last resort of finance for capital expenditure. . . after other sources such as departmental asset sales and accumulated cash;
- any proposal for a capital injection in a department. . . should demonstrate that the level of taxpayers' funds is inadequate for the replacement of the core assets and hence financing from the current balance sheet is not possible; and
- the level of Revenue Crown represents a purchase decision by Ministers on the level of Outputs required, and that Revenue Crown should not normally be altered as a result of changes in capital charge or depreciation expenses following a capital injection or withdrawal."[15]

Prior to the reforms, increases in service levels had been met almost entirely from commensurate increases in funding.

Government Balance Sheet

The publication of a conventional balance sheet for the New Zealand Government is a unique feature

[15]Cabinet Committee on Expenditure Control and Revenue, *Minutes of Cabinet Committee on Expenditure Control and Revenue* (ECR (94)162 and (94)M26/1), meeting held on August 2, 1994.

of the reforms, although subunits of the Government and one Australian state have previously run an accrual accounting system. Although the United States has not produced such a balance sheet, much pioneering work in developing different balance sheet concepts at government and national level has attempted to account for major items such as pension liabilities and investment in education. The movement toward accrual accounting in a growing number of countries is likely to see the increasing development of balance sheets for the Government entity.

While establishing the balance sheet involved a great deal of work, it was a fairly conventional accounting exercise that arose as a natural consequence of the basic performance management framework, which necessitated accounting for the full resource costs of output production. Valuation problems were generally dealt with in conventional and pragmatic ways. Although the procedures were routine, it was very important to use great care in interpreting the actual meaning of a government balance sheet. Properly interpreted, however, it was a valuable addition to the information base used by economists and others in assessing the financial performance and position of the Government. The underlying information systems provide new information superior to that in the national statistical data collection to support the system of national accounts. The balance sheet can also indicate movements in net worth caused by shifts in the balance between capital consumption and new investment. It can provide an indicator of whether the Government is running down its estate in order to maintain current consumption.

At the time of publication of the first balance sheet,[16] Ruth Richardson, the Minister of Finance, emphasized its importance as a contribution to the assessment of future taxation burdens required to support government spending and intergenerational transfers of wealth and income arising from fiscal policy. However, it is important to remember that in a real economic sense, the power of the Government to tax its citizens provides a guarantee of revenue that is not available to a private sector company. It is impossible to value this "asset," and to try to do so drowns the other information in the balance sheet and deprives it of meaning. On the liabilities side, the value of future social welfare obligations is, similarly, a large item that is very difficult to quantify.

These questions of future revenue and expenditure flows are of vital interest in economic management; but it was decided they are not usefully dealt with in the context of a balance sheet, which focuses on other questions that are important in their own right, and had largely been ignored.

[16]New Zealand Government, *Financial Statements of the Government of New Zealand for the six months ended 31 December 1991*.

External Accountability and the Fiscal Responsibility Act

Parliamentary Scrutiny

There are three distinct elements in the work of Parliament and its committees in scrutinizing the financial management of the executive:

- scrutiny of the Government's intentions for the current year as expressed in its budget proposals;
- examination of the actual performance of departments, as reported in their annual reports and financial statements and by comparison with the plans laid a year earlier; and
- examination of the performance of state-owned enterprises and other nondepartmental government entities.

This cycle of scrutiny emphasizes the comparison of actual performance with planned performance. Previously there had been a considerable disjuncture between the budget process and the scrutiny of the Government's ex post financial statements. Different concepts and information systems were included in the budgetary and financial reporting processes, and there was little, if any, emphasis on the performance of the departments themselves. The Public Finance Act, passed in 1989, brought major improvements in reporting to Parliament in terms of requiring the ex post and ex ante information to converge and to be related to issues of performance. This began at the departmental level and progressed to cover the Government as a whole. From 1992, these requirements were extended to the whole of the activities of the Government, and not solely to those of the departments.

Fiscal Responsibility Act

The Fiscal Responsibility Act and related amendments to the Public Finance Act were both passed in June 1994 and substantially revised and developed the requirements for fiscal reporting in a way that produced major advances in the transparency and accountability of fiscal policy decisions. The Act specifies requirements for information and policy documents, while establishing statutory accountability for the Government and Treasury for providing that information. In addition, it specifies principles of sound fiscal policy with the intention that any fiscal strategy proposed by the Government should be able to be assessed in relation to those criteria through the information provided. It also provides for more open budgetary processes.

The Act was sponsored by the Minister of Finance at the time, Ruth Richardson, who subsequently steered the Act through the House from the position of chair of Parliament's Finance and Expenditure Committee after she had left the Cabinet following the 1993 election. She promoted the Act as a response to long-standing concerns that she and her supporters had about the difficulties with fiscal policy. On too many occasions, short-term political pressures had overridden the requirements of a sound medium-term financial strategy. By the time the Act was passed, New Zealand had 12 years of political and administrative difficulties in recovering from the fiscal problems of the early 1980s. She saw it as imperative that New Zealand have a credible medium-term fiscal policy underpinned by a sustainable debt situation. Tensions between an unsustainable fiscal policy and a monetary policy that was growing in credibility under the newly independent central bank had caused macroeconomic imbalances from the late 1980s until 1991/92, and it was seen as vital to establish credible long-term fiscal policy.

One of the impulses for the Fiscal Responsibility Act was concern about fiscal decision making after the introduction of the Mixed Member Proportional Representation in 1996, which may lead to coalition or minority government. The experience of getting Cabinet agreement to sound fiscal policy with majority governments had been sufficiently difficult that the prospect of coalitions and minority governments maintaining political cohesion at the expense of fiscal policy was a concern to policymakers.

A further impetus for the Act came from concerns, following several recent elections, that the public had not been fully informed about the fiscal outlook during the election campaign. As a consequence, both the Labour Party after 1984 and the National Party after 1990 found themselves with a fiscal situation that forced them to make major changes in their policy platforms. New Zealand's Ombudsman had stated that this unsatisfactory situation needed to be addressed. The Act provides for full exposure of the fiscal situation in the period leading up to an election.

From a theoretical standpoint, the Act seeks to address possible biases in democratic processes toward outcomes that are not in accord with voters' interests or may be inefficient in serving them. This can arise because of the information and transactions costs inherent in offsetting the influences of special interests and prospective short-term gains over the wider public interest in the longer term. Future generations of taxpayers may be underrepresented by today's voters, and information is poor as regards the deadweight losses imposed by taxation in particular. The Act tries to counteract these biases by requiring full exposure of the longer-term implications of current fiscal strategy. It also imposes stable and predictable budgetary processes. It had been the view of the Treasury, in particular, that some of the fiscal difficulties of the 1980s had been exacerbated by budgetary processes that, at times, had allowed for ad hoc decision making on the basis of information that was soon to be revised.

Projections

Projections up to 10 years of major fiscal variables are required and, while these are not forecasts, they help to indicate the extent to which the tax burden is being shifted into the future. They also show the long-term implications of policies that are of a long-term contractual nature, such as the retirement benefit programs that have caused so much political stress and fiscal difficulty in the last 20 years.

Information Systems

The Act requires that the same information systems are used for budgeting and reporting of the Government's finances. The Generally Accepted Accounting Principles are required to be used throughout the public sector, and this has the effect of extending accrual accounting comprehensively throughout the public sector. Under another Act of Parliament, the Financial Reporting Act, the Accounting Standards Review Board has been established, and oversees the development of new accounting standards. In New Zealand, the same accounting standards apply to both the Government and the private sector, although standards that are specific to public sector issues can be developed within that regime.

Targets and Guidelines

After an extensive debate and review of experiences of mandatory fiscal targets, particularly in the United States, Parliament inserted into the Act five principles for responsible fiscal management:

- reducing total Crown debt to prudent levels by achieving operating surpluses every year until a prudent level of debt has been obtained;
- maintaining total Crown debt at a prudent level by ensuring that on average operating expenses of the Crown do not exceed operating revenue;
- achieving and maintaining levels of Crown net worth that provide a buffer against adverse future events;
- prudent management of the fiscal risks facing the Crown; and
- the pursuit of policies consistent with a reasonable degree of predictability about the level and stability of tax rates for future years.

Departures from these principles must be transparent and temporary, although the Act does not ultimately prohibit the Government from having any fiscal policy it can get the support of a majority in Parliament for. Requirements about decision processes and information and the need to explain departures from the specified fiscal principles would constrain a government that could not provide a comprehensive and credible explanation of why it was departing from those principles.

While some proposals were made in the select committee process for the adoption of mandatory fiscal targets, the balance of judgment was that the incentives that these created for distortionary fiscal decisions, such as moving activities off budget, outweighed the possible benefits of stronger commitments to sound fiscal principles.

Reporting Requirements

As far as the Government's exposure of fiscal information processes to Parliament is concerned, the Act requires a structured sequence of reports. The Government is required to have a budget policy statement presented to Parliament three months before the deadline for the budget. This sets out the Government's intentions for the coming budget within a longer-term framework and by reference to the fiscal principles specified in the Act. This establishes the parameters for the forthcoming budget. The intention is to initiate the budget debate at the macroeconomic and strategic levels in order to set guidelines for the detail to come. A fiscal strategy report is required at the time of the budget, which compares the details of the budget with what was proposed in the budget policy statement. Subsequently, Parliament is given regular economic and fiscal updates in addition to the special report prior to an election. All of these reports, of which details are laid out below, are referred to Parliament's Finance and Expenditure Committee for scrutiny.

Budget Policy Statement

The budget policy statement is to be published by March 31 of each year (the fiscal year begins on July 1). It provides for the following:

- specifies the Government's long-term objectives for fiscal policy and some specified fiscal variables such as operating expenses, the operating surplus or deficit, total debt, and net worth;
- sets strategic priorities for the three following financial years that will guide the preparation of the current year's budget;
- states the Government's intentions for the next three years with regard to specified fiscal variables;
- assesses the consistency of these intentions with principles of responsible fiscal policy specified in the Act;
- specifies the reasons for any departure from these principles; and
- assesses the consistency of the current intentions with those of the previous budget policy statement.

Fiscal Strategy Report

The fiscal strategy report must be tabled on the day of the first Appropriation bill for the fiscal year, which effectively means on the day of the budget. It must include an assessment of the consistency of the current economic and fiscal situation with the information and intentions presented previously in the budget strategy report, and an amended set of intentions where circumstances have changed. It must also include projections of key fiscal variables for the next ten years, illustrating progress toward the longer-term strategic goals contained in the budget policy statement and explaining any discrepancies from earlier intentions as assessed by comparison with principles of responsible fiscal management.

Economic and Fiscal Update

The economic and fiscal update report must be prepared by the Treasury and tabled on the day of the first Appropriation Act. It must also have the following items:

- contain economic and fiscal forecasts for the current fiscal year and the two following years, and state the last day on which information was entered into the report;
- provide forecasts for the economy covering the outlook for the next three years for GDP, consumer prices, employment, unemployment, and the balance of payments current account, and state the significant underlying assumptions;
- provide three-year fiscal forecasts, including forecast financial statements of the Government in the full detail described above;
- incorporate all government decisions and other circumstances that have a material effect on the fiscal outlook; and
- be accompanied by a statement of responsibility signed by the Minister of Finance and the Secretary to the Treasury.

Current Year Fiscal Update

The current year fiscal update contains the latest fiscal information for the financial year and expectations for the Government's financial statements for the year ending in June, and is required after the end of March, which is when the Government is making its final budget decisions.

Half-Year Economic and Fiscal Update

The essential purpose of the half-year economic and fiscal update is to provide Parliament with an update of the main elements of the reports described above together with a statement of responsibility. It is required to be published in December.

The Fiscal Responsibility Act's provisions are aimed at the relationship between the executive and Parliament, whereas the 1994 amendments to the Public Finance Act developed the estimates documents accompanying the budget by setting out requirements for information from the departments.

It should be noted that there may be several votes to a department, and one minister may be responsible for several votes—not necessarily in the same department—but each vote has only one minister. In addition to these ministerial responsibilities for votes, which reflect the purchase interest, each department has a minister who is named the "responsible minister" and is concerned with the ownership interest. The estimates document must, in respect of each vote, show the following information:

- the proposed expenses and liabilities to be incurred in respect of each of the seven types of appropriation;
- the classes of output to be purchased by the Government;
- the linkages between the classes of outputs and the Government's desired outcomes;
- the intended purposes of appropriations other than for output purchase;
- projections of appropriations for several years;
- net worth at the start and forecast for the end of the year for the department;
- net worth information for any state-owned entities or Crown entities for which the vote minister is responsible; and
- expenses and liabilities arising in respect of other sources of legislative authority, for example, permanent legislative authority.

Forecast Financial Statements of Departments

In a separate document, presented to Parliament by the Minister of Finance on behalf of the responsible ministers of each department at the time of the budget, each department's financial forecasts for the coming year contain the following:

- statement of financial position; operating statement; and cash flow, with significant assumptions;
- statement of objectives specifying classes of outputs, expected revenue and expense for each class, and financial performance objectives agreed with the responsible minister;
- statement of accounting policies; and
- statement of responsibility by the chief executive who is responsible for the forecast and attests that the information in them is consistent with the information contained in the estimates document presented to Parliament at the same time.

Other Documents

The Public Finance Act also requires annual and half-yearly financial statements; monthly financial statements by the Government; departmental financial statements in the same format as the forecast information above; and annual reports and financial statements by nondepartmental entities of the Government—the so-called Crown entities.

Assessing the Results

Previous sections have included comments on the effectiveness of elements of the system, but a few additional remarks are relevant.

The information available to members of Parliament has been significantly improved as a result of these reforms, although it has taken two sets of revisions to arrange the information in a form that politicians want. Amendments to parliamentary standing orders, which were designed to bring the parliamentary process into better alignment with the budget and financial reporting cycles, appear to have had some success in differentiating between the scrutiny of budgets for the forthcoming year and the evaluation of performance in the previous year. This is an important contribution to improvements in performance evaluation.

The budget process is now more transparent, and it is evident that resource switching has occurred, with the specific purpose of giving effect to ministerial decisions. However, unambiguous evidence of the extent to which these shifts were attributable to the financial management reforms is more difficult to determine. David Caygill, the Minister of Finance between 1988 and 1990, who introduced the Public Finance Act, expressed his satisfaction that the reforms had provided much improved information for budget decision making. Ruth Richardson, Minister of Finance between 1991 and 1993, is unequivocal in her view that the reforms to core government administration gave her the "tools" to put the "lid" on public expenditure and to shift priorities. The current Minister of Finance, Bill Birch, believes that the Government's abilities to prioritize and control spending have been enhanced by the reforms. His comments[17] are significant because he initially was not a champion of the reforms and also had extensive experience of the old system when he was a senior minister in the Government in the early 1980s.

Despite the primacy of the criterion of efficiency, departments have, over several years, not received compensation for the effects of price changes. There is little evidence, however, to suggest that the volume or quality of output has diminished, other than as a result of explicit policy decisions. In addition, at a lower level, there are observable improvements in the use of assets generally, and of working capital and cash in particular.

The reforms have had two effects on the management of the fiscal position. First, the arrangements that now operate at the departmental level facilitate expenditure control by ministers. The capacity to restrain expenditure is evidenced at the aggregate level by the decline in expenditure (on a cash flow basis) for operating activities for the year ended June 30, 1992, where cash flows declined by approximately $NZ 1.5 billion on a base of $NZ 31 billion. Second, the improved transparency of the fiscal position has helped, at the aggregate level, to ensure that decisions are made with greater recognition of their long-term impact.

The acceptance of the reforms can be gauged from the results of the review of state sector reforms instituted by the National Government after it took office in 1990. This review was headed by Basil Logan, the retired head of IBM in New Zealand, and was completed in November 1991. It broadly supported the direction of reforms and expressed little concern with any of the principal elements of the system; the review's major conclusions referred to the strengthening of certain elements of the system. Logan found that the definition of outputs needed tightening, the incentive framework needed development, the recruitment and development of top executives needed particular attention, and there was some concern that the autonomy granted to departmental chief executives and their tight accountability to their ministers might weaken the capacity of the Government to act in a coordinated and collegial way.

Some ministers have said that the Cabinet has not taken a strategic grip on the system, with the result that the departmental heads are too influential in the setting of their output requirements and the Government's desired outcomes. Some departmental heads also complain that the Treasury is looking for too much detail about their management plans.

Early evidence suggests that the improved information now made available does assist the Government in its macromanagement of the economy. Faced with choices at the margin in relation to government spending, ministers can make decisions with a clearer sense of their impact. They have a better specification of exactly what services departments will provide, which provides a better basis for analyzing the effect of those services on the Government's strategic goals. They are also able to obtain much better information on the actual delivery of services by departments.

In terms of the effects that decentralized financial management had on the Government's wider goals, the state-owned enterprise policy has had a much larger influence on the performance of a substantial part of the economy. In the remainder of the Government, the influences on effectiveness and efficiency have been significant by many criteria, but their effects are inherently harder to gauge than in purely commercial activities.

[17]Rt. Hon. Bill Birch, Minister of Finance, Speech delivered at the Deloitte/National Business Review Budget breakfast on May 29, 1995 (Wellington).

X Lessons of Reform

Big Changes Can Be Rapid Changes

Making major, root-and-branch changes in public sector management raises a number of risks. The bigger those changes, the greater, of course, is the risk. Whether a country whose government management systems are failing to produce results is better advised to plan a giant leap forward, or to set out on a path of reform that may take ten years or more, is a question without a general answer. Ideally, careful planning of change management strategies enables risks to be contained, but the reality is that unexpected events occur and trends can turn adverse. Taking longer does not necessarily make change easier. New Zealand is no exception, and developments learned, demonstrated that comprehensive and fundamental change in a short period of time is possible. This section summarizes a few lessons in implementation that were learned. It does not repeat the points about the implementation of aspects of the system that were covered in the previous sections.

Lessons in Implementation

Recognize the Problem

For reform to occur, there must be acceptance that there is a problem, agreement about its solution, and preparedness to commit to a process of implementation that may have to overcome many obstacles before producing much in the way of visible results. Understandably, these conditions are rare.

In New Zealand, key ministers and the leadership of the bureaucracy were enthusiastic for change; advisors had been preparing proposals for several years before the political opportunity arose for ministers to launch a reform program following the 1984 election. The basic outlines of the system were established immediately after the election in a few hours of urgent meetings between senior ministers and key advisers. Following these meetings, a program for implementation was put in place over the next two years that changed the way in which every government agency was managed. The introduction of the new financial management systems took 18 months and was introduced six months ahead of schedule. This pace of change was possible only because of the general recognition of the need for change in government administration, in an environment where other large changes were occurring and in which there was little support for the status quo.

However, as the reforms progressed, New Zealand remained in a very difficult financial and political situation. Tax reform, increases in all government charges, and the introduction of charges for many previously free services had boosted government revenue to the point of arousing considerable political resistance. Government expenditure on support for industry had been removed. Government businesses converted to state-owned enterprises were paying dividends and taxes out of profits for the first time and were not benefiting from government funding of their investment programs. Government administration was being squeezed. Welfare support for citizens had been withdrawn from the middle classes and targeted to those in need. All this did not, however, eliminate the problem of a large structural fiscal deficit.

Furthermore, some ministers were dissatisfied about the regimes for setting public sector wages, which put politicians in the position of having to take direct responsibility for detailed industrial relations issues in a highly politicized atmosphere. Substantial wage increases had resulted, and these had contributed to a damaging wage explosion in the economy as a whole. Some ministers were also dissatisfied with their departmental heads' perceived lack of freedom in making sensible choices about inputs.

Over the whole of the period of change in New Zealand, there was a general move to undertake reform of institutions that had been largely unchanged for a long time. Deregulation, removal of protection from imports, and the removal of subsidies in the private sector, together with measures to expand the corporate tax base and high interest rates resulting from both deregulation of financial markets and firm monetary policy, meant that the private sector was being heavily squeezed in a general period of restructuring and retrenchment. The pressures for restructuring in the private sector and the exposure of incredible inefficiencies in the parts of the corporatized public sector, all added to an environment in which proposals for reform would, in principle, fall on fertile soil. However, the reforms attracted a certain degree of political unpopularity, which, from time to time, made it difficult for politicians and their advisers to sustain the momentum, and maintain the comprehensiveness of the reforms that they knew were necessary.

Many commentators have concluded from this experience that a serious problem is required to provide the political foundations for major public reform. If this is so, countries are destined to have long periods of slow decline in the effectiveness of public institutions punctuated by periodic major reforms. Over time, this will produce far worse outcomes than a system that is constantly upgrading itself because it has the incentives, ideas, and resources to do so. Decentralized systems subject to pressures to perform can upgrade constantly. It might also be suggested from New Zealand's experience that ideas and political and bureaucratic leadership might effect change even without a crisis. Certainly there are many countries in crisis that have not succeeded in implementing or even attempted to introduce programs to make their governments more effective.

Solve a Sequence of Real Problems

There is a natural temptation for the designers of government financial management systems to seek to implement a grand design. The realities of day-to-day government are such that grand designs rarely capture the interest of politicians, even when they have real problems they want solved. While it is important to have an end-point in mind, and principles that ensure that inconsistencies are not built into the system, the change management program should emphasize the solution to the sequence of real problems. This can improve the design and produce early payoffs that will justify the costs and gain political support for maintaining the pace of reform.

The output-based budget information was used even when it was available only in a rough form to help ministers set priorities for expenditure when putting together an extremely difficult budget in 1990. This won support for reform from senior ministers who had previously distanced themselves from change.

Political Commitment Is Necessary at Key Points

While it may not have been necessary to have the commitment of the Prime Minister to the program of reform, it could not have proceeded in the face of his opposition. Nor could reform have been accomplished without the leadership of the Minister of Finance and other key ministers involved in fiscal policy and public administration. Aside from steering the necessary legislative proposals through the Government and Parliament, the implementation program required little direct input from such senior political figures; but it was important that they show their support on several occasions, particularly to the top management of the civil service.

It might have been possible to introduce the financial reforms without legislative change, but it was thought desirable to pass legislation and thereby make clear the purpose and philosophy of the changes, as well as the technicalities. This clarity helped to emphasize the message that the Government was insisting on changes to public sector management. This relatively low level of top political input was due in large part to the fact that energetic opposition from the Government's political opponents was limited; indeed, the reform program was started by one Government and completed by another.

Leadership from Heads of Departments Is Essential

The chief executives of the government departments and the heads of the central agencies were committed to change. There are always opportunities to frustrate the intent of the scheme; it was also essential, therefore, to find and maintain the support of influential officials inside departments to see that the momentum of change was maintained. A passive attitude by a chief executive will lead to unsatisfactory results, even though there may be nominal compliance with the requirements.

Do Not Relax Central Controls Too Soon

The central agencies took a major role in developing the output definitions at the outset. For practical purposes, they and the Minister of Finance had a strong influence on the outputs because they had to advise the Government on whether to release departments from input controls. To achieve this, the Public Finance Act provided for departments to move singly from detailed input controls to outputs, and to freedom from most controls. A two-year deadline for conversion was set, and proved to be enough time for the Government to deal individually with the departments and appraise their readiness for the transition—particularly those departments where the necessary internal systems development had not proceeded under the old regime. This avoided the danger of removing input controls without having in place the new system for output control. The risk was a real one. Some chief executives tried to gain excessive freedom through vague output definitions. In one case, a department sought to have only one output for a huge and complex government agency. The result would have been no control whatsoever.

Managers Will Welcome Change

Irrespective of attitudes at the top of the system, individuals who know where to find the real waste and inefficiency in government administration are to be found farther down the organization's hierarchy. The New Zealand system is designed to empower such officials to make changes in the way they manage their staff and other resources, and increase their responsiveness to customer requirements.

It is common for resistance to change to come from officials who are comfortable with the old system, and in many departments, it proved necessary to change key individuals in the financial management area. The change management program will pass through at least three phases and will probably require different skills at varying times that will not always be found within the same individuals.

First, a heavy effort is needed in conceptualization, planning, and strategy. Second, the early implementation phase involves very different skills: in organizing large numbers of people, some of whom are unsure of themselves and unsettled by the change but who must be motivated to devise rapid and practical solutions to problems. Inevitably, problems will develop and remedial intervention will be needed. The whole system of government finance is being reworked or replaced, but the basic functions of the system still have to operate satisfactorily, day by day.

Third, once the system has begun to operate, the emphasis moves to decentralized activities: seeking improvement through technical development, staff training, learning from errors, sharing best practice, and so on. Managers at this stage begin to see all the new possibilities for improving management through using the systems instead of being preoccupied with the difficulties of installation.

However, some of this continuing change requires a change in individuals' habits and attitudes, which often do not shift as rapidly as the systems themselves. Having an accrual accounting system in place is of limited use if staff are still accumulating invoices at the end of the financial year to be carried over into the next year. Constant reinforcement of the needs to change—and of the rewards from change—is necessary.

Create Incentives for Change

Departmental heads saw the removal of controls over their inputs as a positive change, and this type of motivation can help to implement the reforms. Chief executives also took note of the fact that the law made them the chief finance officer of their department. This led to widespread hiring of qualified professional accountants and brought departmental finance officers into senior executive teams producing a marked upgrade in the quality of financial management. Financial managers in departments took pride in raising the systems up to the necessary standard, in return for which managers in their departments were given greater freedom to manage. No department wanted to be the last one to be approved for transition to the new system.

Communicate the Objectives of Changes

The reforms caused extra work for many people whose motivation depended on their understanding of the changes, and of the benefits they would bring for the Government as a whole and for their operations in particular. Many senior managers throughout the bureaucracy had never been particularly interested in financial management and needed to be persuaded to give the issue the high priority essential if the changes were to succeed. Once senior ministers had made their intentions clear, a great effort was required from the Treasury and financial managers throughout the Government, the Accountants Society, the Audit Office, and others, to disseminate objectives and requirements at each stage, and to translate the general objectives of reform into specific details for each agency. Departments involved with public interest groups needed communications programs to explain the process and the manner in which the public would be affected.

Decentralize Technical Accounting Issues

Consistent with the decentralizing principles of the regime, Parliament and the Treasury avoided directing the detailed accounting practices of individual departments. The generally accepted accounting principles hold departments to standard conventions in making these decisions, and the lack of strict comparability that might have arisen from the variation across departments was a small price to pay for the efficiencies and incentives of imposing the obligations directly on the departments. Any inconsistencies can be rectified later if they appear to be material. For example, the definition of policy analysis varied across departments, which caused confusion when politicians interrogated the system as to total expenditure on the policy analysis category. The Treasury is now coordinating the development of more uniform definitions.

Accept the Allocation of Senior Management Time to Change

The transition from the role of a traditional departmental head to a new decentralized management role required chief executives to spend much time overseeing the development of the new management systems that would eventually enable them to change their role and responsibilities, and would in time become routine.

During this phase, dissatisfaction was occasionally expressed by both managers and ministers, at the degree of effort being directed at management reform while some of the traditional functions of policy advice and representation received less attention than previously. This was a temporary phase for most departments, although some have continued to require major management developments that have called on considerable chief executive time.

Manage Transitional Risks Carefully

Opponents of reform will seize upon any early problems or difficulties in implementation associated with the new system, highlighting the risks inherent in making major changes to management and financial systems. New accounting systems may not work perfectly at first, and it is not always feasible to run the old and new systems in parallel. The early information in the new formats had inconsistencies and errors that took time to rectify. Managers exercising new freedoms made a few mistakes that attracted attention.

Managing these risks involves using common sense in anticipating them, and intervening quickly to limit the damage and correct the problem. The importance assumed by problems is also diminished if the overall program is producing early results.

Managing Change at Departmental Level Is Critical for Success

This report does not discuss the details of managing change within a government department. It is important to strongly emphasize, however, how critical a factor change in management is in the implementation of comprehensive management reform.

The new system shifted the responsibility for management onto departmental chiefs, therefore, success or failure depended largely on the chiefs' response. They became personally responsible for managing strategy, operations, personnel, and finance to achieve results that are public knowledge. Some officials who rose to top positions under the previous system were not capable of assuming such full personal responsibility. Their success had come from policy advice, diplomacy, and seniority rather than skills of strategic leadership and the management of complex organizations. Below these senior officials were some deputies and assistants who had been promoted into management for extra status and greater reward, but were not skilled—and sometimes not interested—in management.

A high class of leadership, motivation, communication, and management skill from the top of the organization was necessary to enable staff who were resistant to change to become comfortable with it. Greater freedom to create their own incentives for change enabled senior managers to implement it more effectively.

Assuming competent top management is in place, the change process involves the following elements:

- A clear mission for the organization that is absorbed throughout the organization; such a mission would comprise corporate values that guide the organization's behavior in respect of staff, clients, the public, and politicians; and its commitments to the quality of what it does and how it does it; and strategic plans that define and prioritize important achievements in terms of outputs and of the development of the organization as a healthy entity.
- Operational plans that, first, translate strategies into detailed agreements assigning responsibility for results and the allocation of resources, and, second, specify information flows internally and externally; incorporating communication strategies that ensure that all the above is known and understood, and that the staff affected are involved in setting goals and making plans and are committed to their achievement.
- Enabling systems that allocate and develop resources, ensure quality, specify results, monitor achievements, and motivate staff for performance and innovation; support for such systems would include appropriate finance, management assurance, quality management, information technology, and asset management; and human resource management that aims to nurture the development of staff with the competencies necessary if the organization is to provide constantly improving services with increased efficiency.

XI Contribution of Government Management Reform to New Zealand's Economic Adjustment

Impact of Reforms on Adjustment

As New Zealand's reforms to its systems and processes of managing the Government were a central component of a wider strategy of economic adjustment, an assessment of their effects should therefore take account of their contribution in that context after 1984. The reforms had an impact on adjustment through their interrelated effects on changing the role of government, macroeconomic and fiscal policy, the setting of policy priorities, the institutional implementation of policies, and the increasing efficiency of government entities. A problem in seeking to analyze and quantify the nature and extent of these influences is that it is impossible to know what would have occurred if the reforms had not been implemented or had been altered. It is possible, however, to make a rough correlation of the reforms with the fiscal outcomes, and draw certain inferences about their contribution.

Fiscal and Economic Trends

The overall fiscal developments can be seen at a glance in Charts 2–6.

The deficit-to-GDP ratio chart shows three different concepts of the deficit. The key point to note in the period in which the government reforms were introduced is the divergence between financial balance and the cash balance, reflecting receipts from privatization. The expanding gap between the primary balance and the financial balance reflects the build-up of debt. The financial balance shows the steady progress of the Labour Government resolving the earlier fiscal crisis between 1984 and 1990, but also the loss of fiscal control in the months before the 1990 election. The effects of the tough 1991 budget and the recovery in the economy from late 1991 explains the rapid turnaround after that time.

The fiscal effects of the privatization program can be clearly seen in the movements in the cash deficit. An interesting feature in the deficit chart is that the spikes in the deficit coincide with election years. During the years in which the Labour Party was reelected, in 1987, and the National Party was reelected, in 1993, no such deterioration occurred. On both these occasions, Ministers of Finance successfully resisted pressures to expand spending.

An essential feature of the 1991 budget was to address an agenda of social policy reform that the previous Labour Government had avoided. The social welfare benefit levels were cut, and very tough constraints on costs were placed across government administrative activities. Structural reforms were introduced through many areas, including the delivery of government services in health, education, science, and elsewhere to restrain spending and create strong incentives for efficiency. The national Government was also committed to solving the fiscal problem on the expenditure side rather than raising taxes.

In interpreting the expenditure chart, it should be noted that the measure of expenditure includes debt servicing and investment transactions that net out the proceeds of privatization after 1987. Removing the effects of privatization proceeds from expenditure reveals that the share of expenditure to GDP fell from 42 percent to 35 percent between 1991 and 1994.

The key points to note in Chart 4 are the sharp declines in the revenue-to-GDP ratio following the tax-based incomes policy in the early 1980s, and in the recession in 1991, at which time there were also lagged effects on tax revenues from the weak corporate balance sheets resulting from the stock market crash. There is also evidence that corporate tax avoidance activities were unusually extensive at the time, as it took several years to adapt the tax laws to close off new opportunities for avoidance arising from the internationalization of the economy.

As shown in Chart 5, the growth rate of the real economy was volatile during the period. The major influences on fiscal policy coming from movements in the economy were movements in tax revenues and some social transfer payments, as noted in Charts 4 and 5. In very broad terms, the effects of these feedbacks between fiscal aggregates and movements in the economy were to create virtuous and vicious cycles in fiscal behavior.

A vicious cycle emerged in the second term of the Labour Government, from 1987 to 1990. The shock

Chart 2. Deficits as Percent of GDP

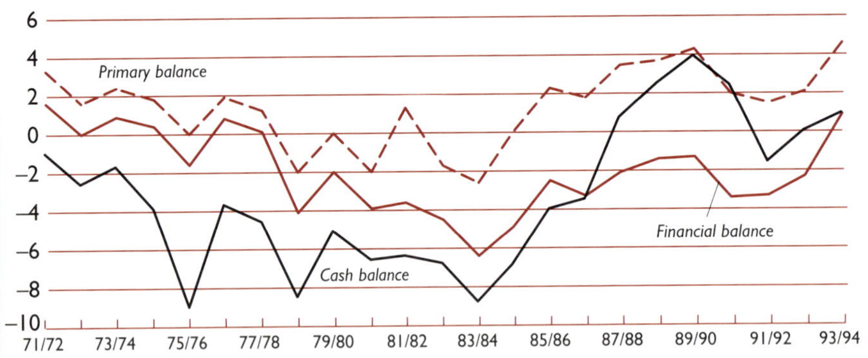

Source: New Zealand Institute of Economic Research.

to the economy from the stock market crash worsened a fiscal situation that was still weak, notwithstanding the improvements that had been made from 1984 to 1987. From then on, any further bad news in fiscal policy, as emerged on several occasions, was quickly translated into rises in interest rates and the exchange rate, thus tending to slow down the economy. This was caused by the imbalance between fiscal and monetary policies made apparent because of the growing credibility of the newly independent central bank and the deregulated financial markets. These negative effects on the economy, in turn, caused further fiscal deterioration. The difficulties of gaining political support for tightening fiscal stance in those circumstances added further strain to the Government's budget decision making and its political credibility.

After 1988, fiscal consolidation stalled because of the weak economy and sharp ideological differences within the Labour Government over whether social policy expenditure should be subjected to the same degree of radical reform that other classes of expenditure, together with the tax system, had been exposed to since 1984. Reform continued, however, in other social policy areas, with an aggressive privatization program, in particular. Ultimately, these beneficial effects through improved efficiencies and reduction of debt-service payments were insufficient

Chart 3. Government Expenditure as Percent of GDP

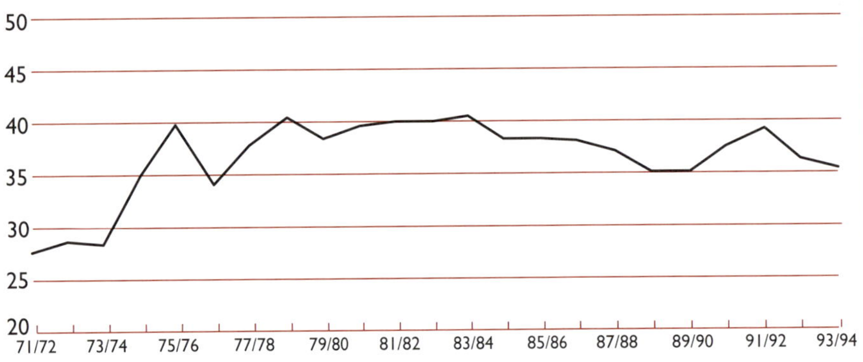

Source: New Zealand Institute of Economic Research.

Chart 4. Taxes as Percent of GDP

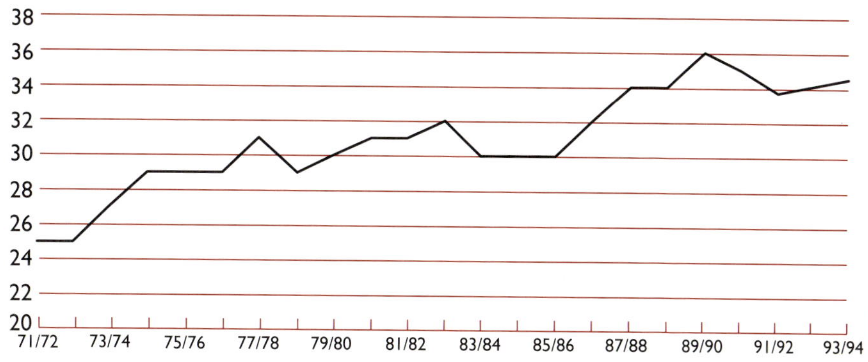

Source: New Zealand Institute of Economic Research.

to offset the effects of reluctance to make fiscal reforms in social policy and the effects of the weakening economy driven by the real wealth effect of the share market crash and the consequent commercial property market malaise. Also, in 1990, the terms of trade fell, weakening further the economy. Tax revenues weakened, and social transfer payments rose. At the end of the Labour Government's term, in 1990, when it was defeated at the polls, it increased social expenditure, which was a partial contributor to the fiscal expansion that set the scene for the tough budget in 1991. This cycle of fiscal deterioration, economic weakening, and political difficulties for the Government was reinforced by the concurrent decline in business confidence that caused weaker investment and retrenchment.

Chart 5. GDP Annual Growth
(In percent)

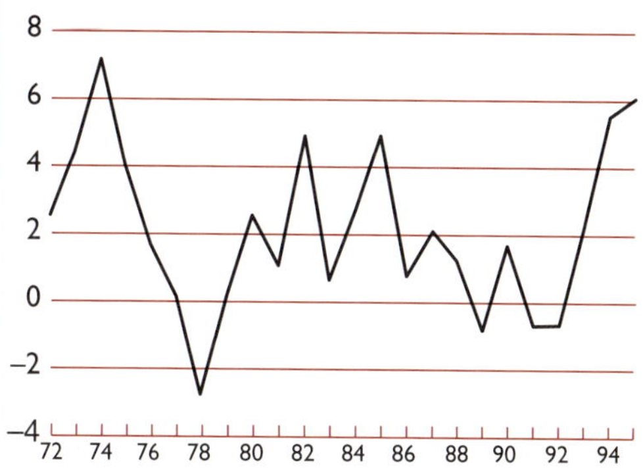

Source: New Zealand Institute of Economic Research.

This vicious cycle continued through 1991. In that year, a very tough budget restored credibility to the fiscal outlook in spite of the recession. In late 1991, the economy turned around sharply and over the ensuing years, a virtuous cycle of economic improvement and fiscal improvement has been in place.

Both cycles were reinforced with a time lag through the effects of the fiscal situation on the debt burden. After 1991, nominal interest rates fell, reflecting reducing inflationary expectations, despite the improving economy, and an improving ability to service debt, and subsequent exchange rate strengthening reduced the costs of servicing debt, while the reduction in the deficit slowed the growth of debt and eventually caused it to shrink. Debt movements are illustrated in Chart 6.

With strong constraints on spending in place and a growing economy, the fiscal turnaround has been such that the Government is making substantial tax cuts in 1996, while maintaining a sound fiscal outlook with debt reductions, and with the net worth in the Government's balance sheet moving toward a positive balance in two years' time.

Associations Between Fiscal Outcomes and Particular Management Reforms

Macroaggregates

Evidence suggests that New Zealand's comprehensive approach to reform made a significant contribution to its gradual return to fiscal balance. There is a clear, temporal association between the improvements in the fiscal position and the implemen-

Chart 6. Net Public Debt as a Percent of GDP

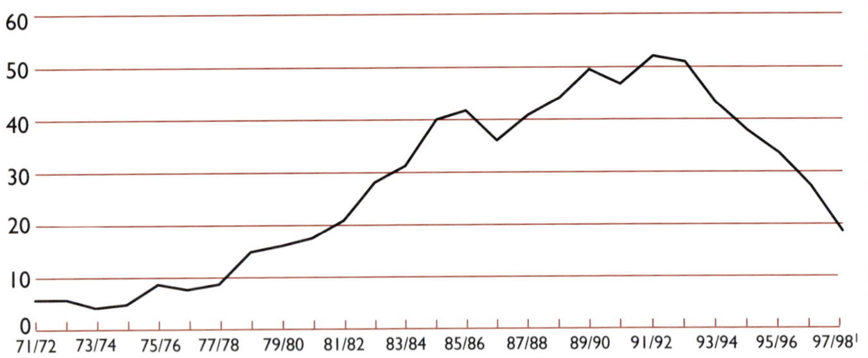

Source: New Zealand Institute of Economic Research.
[1]Author's projections.

tation of the state-owned enterprises policy, in 1986, and the privatization program between 1988 and 1990. There is also an association between the fiscal consolidation in 1991 and the downstream operational impacts effects of structural reforms to many government agencies—the Public Finance Act and the State Sector Act.

The state-owned enterprises policy took resource-hungry, government-owned businesses out of the budget sector and forced them to raise their efficiency, in part by competing for finance in the private sector. Previous management information systems were too poor to permit more than rough impressions from the statistics. The public investment in government-owned businesses was about $NZ 20 billion (compared with a GDP of $NZ 80 billion). They produced 12 percent of GDP, accounted for 17 percent of national investment, and provided no taxes or dividends. Today, the remaining state-owned enterprises provide 5 percent of GDP and pay about $NZ 1 billion in taxes and dividends. They have gone from negative rates of return to full commercial rates of return on resources employed.

Moving such a large volume of assets to the private sector, where they have to earn a normal rate of return on capital and pay taxes and dividends while generally providing better services at lower prices in real terms, apparently had a significant effect on the economy as a whole. Case studies of the telecommunications industry and the electricity corporatization policy bear this out in detail.

Privatization has yielded about $NZ 14 billion in receipts, and although the justification for privatization is the strengthening of incentives for efficiency by changing asset ownership, the impacts on the Government's financial position is readily apparent from the cash deficit in Chart 5.

The decentralized management system and improved budgetary processes within the budget sector enabled the Government to limit the resources available for many government activities that previously had relatively easy access to funds incrementally. This involved central agencies and ministers giving up much of their authority for detailed intervention in the management of government institutions; however, as has already been shown, these controls had not been associated with satisfactory fiscal control overall. In a sense, the center of the Government had to give up the appearance of control in order to gain more of the substance of control.

More Efficient Budgeting

The reform of government management has enabled budgeting to be more efficient, in the sense that it increased the Government's capacity to set goals and priorities for fiscal policy and broadly to maintain them during a period of fiscal stress. The track record can be criticized for being slow, contributing to the recession in 1990 and 1991, and even today, it cannot be claimed that the system is operating to its potential across the Government as a whole. It can be claimed, however, that the new approach to management has established a far better record than the previous systems in delivering budget cuts and constraints while endeavoring to maintain strategic priorities and essential services. The movement in the expenditure-to-GDP ratio noted above and the control on real resources going to administration had never been implemented under the previous system for more than a year or so.

The previous system was more prone to absorb fiscal stress by cutting back on investments and the discretionary resources needed for improved service levels, but maintaining the existing configuration of resources, particularly personnel and nontransparent subsidies. The attempt in the early 1980s to cut 3 percent from the expenditure on government administration was not successful, but cuts of a similar magnitude have routinely been imposed on government departments under the new system. As noted above, there was a 4 percent cut in the cash requirements of the Government in 1991. Ministers report that it is much more feasible to impose cuts or constraints today than previously. The Minister of Finance at the time, Ruth Richardson, has stated that the systems gave her the "tools" to get control of the fiscal aggregates and establish priorities.

Expenditure Composition

Finding statistical evidence as to whether the reforms facilitated the Government's implementation of its policy strategy requires care in interpreting data reflecting changes in directions of spending or the lack of such changes. For example, in an environment of stable policies, a lack of expenditure-switching does not mean that a government is having difficulty in implementing fiscal policy in accordance with its strategic priorities. Over the periods before and after reforms in New Zealand, there were substantial shifts in proportions of expenditure devoted to classes of expenditure. Governments were able to change expenditure directions, particularly in the year after a change of government—1973, 1976, 1985, and 1991. Chart 7 illustrates changes in shares of total expenditure.

What is of particular interest in Chart 7, reflecting whether the reforms facilitated expenditure switching, is that the major switches following the reforms were accompanied by expenditure restraint and a declining deficit. After 1985, there was a decline in the share of fiscal support for industry accompanied by increases in health and education expenditures. In 1991, there were cuts in the share of social services. The expansion of the share of support for industry in the early 1980s was at the expense of the deficit, and occurred at a time when the attempt at across-the-board expenditure cuts was only partially successful. Broadly, the shift in priorities was made more by new spending before reform, more by reallocating spending after reform.

Of course, it cannot be shown statistically that this shift in spending was directly attributable to the new management system as it might just reflect policy priorities. The accompanying pronouncements by the governments at the time, however, supported the view that before the reforms in the early 1980s, the Government did not actually believe in the deficit it created, but found itself unable to do much about it once it had taken decisions to cut taxes and support major industrial development. The last budget of the national Government (1983) was frank about the problem of the deficit, and hoped that recovery in the world economy and possibly reform in the international financial institutions might make it easier to deal with the problem later.

Whatever the aggregate numbers show, the views of the managers involved were that the output-based appropriations, the accountability system, and the freedom granted to managers has considerably sharpened the focus on priorities and the incentives for producing results and operating more efficiently.

Improvements in Efficiency

Difficulty in defining uniform products makes aggregate statistical analysis of efficiency improvements elusive. Quantitative estimates have been made for selected government departments that show significant efficiency gains after the introductions of the State Sector Act and the Public Finance Act. Improvements in efficiency in commercial activities have been quantified and reported in earlier sections.

Fiscal Policy's Contribution to Disequilibrium

Fiscal policy has played a major part in both the creation of New Zealand's former economic problems and the program of adjustment to resolve them. Fiscal policy contributed greatly to creating the major imbalances in the early 1980s that were summarized in Section III. The focus of fiscal strategy had been to stabilize the economy through short-term discretionary adjustments to fiscal settings, to encourage internationally competitive industry with subsides, tax incentives, and investments in commercial enterprises, and to boost social spending, particularly on retirement benefits. Over the next decade, these policies were judged to have failed and were reversed.

Tightening fiscal policy, reforming taxation, and retargeting fiscal instruments to social policy rather than to support for industry proceeded intermittently until 1991, but failure to exert sufficient fiscal control until then slowed the adjustment process and prolonged the recession in the wake of the 1987 world stock market crash. New Zealand experienced the difficulties that many other countries have had in pursuing stabilization and liberalization simultane-

Chart 7. Percentage Shares of Net Government Expenditure

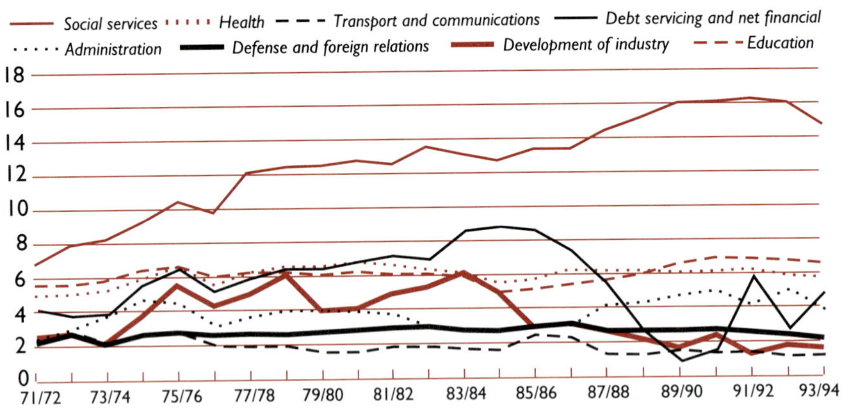

Source: New Zealand Institute of Economic Research.

ously. During the period needed to restore credibility to monetary policy, interest rates were higher than might otherwise have been the case.

In the recovery from a sharp recession in 1991, the economy reached a cyclically high 6 percent real growth rate, with an inflation rate of less than 2 percent in 1994. In 1995, real growth was about 4 percent, and underlying inflation was 2 percent. Unemployment fell from a peak of 11 percent in 1991 to 6 percent in 1995.

Estimates of growth potential are of dubious value in forecasting the future path of output, although they can give some qualified response to the question of how much effect all the reforms have had on growth prospects. In an eclectic study, using a number of econometric techniques, Gibbs (1995) concludes that the sustainable rate of growth currently lies between 3 percent and 4 percent a year. This compares with growth averaging little more than 1.5 percent from 1975 to 1984, while the economy struggled with weaknesses exposed by the two oil shocks. Growth before then had been higher although New Zealand had declined in world rankings of GNP per capita from number 3 in 1950 to number 15 in 1975, and dropped further to number 21 in 1984. Gibbs' estimates show a distinct improvement in growth potential of perhaps 2 percent.

A study by the IMF in 1995 concludes, however, that the growth potential has been raised by a more modest 1 percent. Both these studies are highly dependent on assumptions and methods. Overall, however, it is clear that New Zealand's economic performance is, under current policy settings, positioned near the top on the OECD league table, from a position near the bottom ten years ago before the restructuring began. Time will prove how sustainable the gains in performance are, but today, they are plainly evident.

In 1994, the fiscal deficit in New Zealand was finally eliminated after ten years of difficult political decision making and management reform. The financial risks in the Government's balance sheet are greatly improved, resulting in a new willingness of foreigners to hold New Zealand dollar-denominated debt, and by the hedging of volatility in both international interest and exchange rates and credit and liquidity risk by the NZDMO. The Government's accounts now record contingent liabilities and off-balance-sheet items that are small by comparison with the situation in 1984, when major contingencies were not accounted for.

Improved fiscal management has contributed to a better balance between monetary and fiscal policy, reduced risk from debt levels and is thought by decision makers to have increased the ability for governments to allocate resources to priorities much faster. For example, the allocation of government expenditure excluding debt servicing has shifted markedly away from support for industry, where the Government was needlessly and unsuccessfully involved, and toward vital areas of social policy. The new management regime has helped eliminate waste, and has increased productivity in the production of services in the public sector.

Such assertions are, however, not easy to prove with formal statistical analysis because of problems with data and the issue of the counterfactual noted above. A thorough retrospective evaluation would be timely as a basis for consideration of future development of fiscal policy and administration, and indeed, such work has been initiated. Notwithstanding the absence of a comprehensive evaluation, there is evidence to support some conclusions about the effects of the reforms in regard to fiscal outcomes as regards macroaggregates, expenditure reprioritization, and productivity in service provision.

Looking to the Future

New Zealand has not found it easy to develop and sustain a long-term strategic approach to its economic and social policies, and there is more to be done to help embed this approach to government management. The developments over the last ten years in reforming government management have, however, brought considerable improvements. The development of departmental strategic objectives that are tied back formally into the Government's wider strategic planning processes is a very useful initiative and seen as helpful by managers of government agencies. An independent review commissioned by the Government expressed, however, a degree of concern that the process of setting strategic objectives could be distorted to outweigh the importance of activities favored by the departments themselves, but perhaps not of such significance to the Government's wider strategic goals.

Overall, such formal statistical available evidence and the great majority of opinions of ministers and officials suggest that the reforms to government management greatly changed fiscal policy objectives. It is important, however, not to make exaggerated claims for what the management changes themselves have or could contribute to better performance by the Government. Ultimately, it is the policies, politics, and communications of a government that must be integrated to deliver stable and successful programs. The biggest effects on New Zealand's economic adjustment came from the major policy decisions and the preparedness of successive governments to do unpopular things. A management system can improve the quality of the design and implementation of policies, the information available, and the incentives on the participants, but it is ultimately the policies themselves that make the difference. Good government management makes a substantial contribution to a country's total governance framework, but wider issues of constitutional relations, politics, culture, and national circumstances will determine whether sound principles and systems of management can be instituted, and whether they will work in practice.

As with any country, the benefits of adjustment in the economy in New Zealand can be lost much more easily than they were created. In particular, the hard-won fiscal balance could be at risk as a result of the introduction of mixed member proportional representation in the system for electing representatives to Parliament. This is expected to lead to coalition or minority governments that, it is reasonable to expect, will find it more difficult than the former majority governments did to impose a strategic medium-term objective on fiscal policy. The Fiscal Responsibility Act 1994 was partly a response to this concern, but only time will tell whether it will serve the purpose of setting the sights of New Zealand's decision makers away from the disasters of the past.

XII Relevance of New Zealand's Experience to Other Situations

The writer is commonly asked for comment on the relevance and implications for other countries and for the international organizations of New Zealand's experiences in reforming its systems of government management. These questions center on the adaptability of the system to the problems, objectives, politics, and institutions of other countries and also concern the relationships between the various components of the system and the dynamics of implementing it. Typical questions that are asked are the following:

- Is New Zealand's reform unique to the New Zealand situation?
- Could the performance improvements have been achieved by other means—in particular, by heavy emphasis on evaluation as is found, for example, in Germany?
- What are the implications for the New Zealand approach of the fact that a number of highly successful economies with well-run governments adopt approaches that are completely different in important respects?
- What are the critical conditions for the success of the New Zealand model?
- What are the vital interlinkages between the components of this system, and can other countries pick up particular elements of it and place them in a public sector management system that is otherwise fundamentally different?
- What are the implications of the experience for the work of the IMF?

The purpose of this report has been to present the public sector management reforms in New Zealand as a case study in the response of successive governments in one country to that country's situation and problems. Methodologically, it is very difficult to extrapolate from a particular case study into other situations or to answer the hypothetical question as to whether New Zealand could have improved the performance of its government management by other approaches. We know only the facts of reform and can try only to see the connections between actions and results in that situation. The other questions above are largely hypothetical and the answers must be speculative, but tentative answers are offered below for those for whom the questions are of interest.

Other Countries' Approaches

To examine whether other countries are employing New Zealand's approach to government reform requires some specification of the level of detail at which the comparisons are drawn. At one extreme, no two countries have the same system of public sector management. Many countries use models with common underlying philosophies and a number of common techniques. Countries with a French tradition have distinctively similar characteristics of central control for finance. Countries around the Commonwealth have public sector management systems, particularly financial management systems, that clearly show their origins in the former system of British colonial administration. Some Commonwealth countries maintain management systems that bear a remarkable resemblance to the British system of the 1950s. China, Japan, Korea, and other countries have a system of public administration that is distinctive to the political culture of those societies. In much of Latin America, there is a tradition with traces of Spanish administration from the colonial era. Within each of these traditions, there are examples of countries that have embarked on their own search for greater effectiveness in public administration and adopted ideas that have the same philosophical roots as the New Zealand model, and, in a few cases that acknowledge some influences from the New Zealand experience. The New Zealand system was also considerably influenced by trends and developments in other countries, as was noted earlier in this report.

For readers familiar with public sector reforms in other countries, there are a few general points of comparison that help locate New Zealand's reforms in an international context. The reform of the commercial activities of the Government during the mid- and late 1980s followed the general lines of policy and implementation seen in the United Kingdom, and, to a much lesser extent, in Australia. These activities were placed in new organizational forms that were commercial rather than political objectives. There was arguably no ideological preference for private ownership in principle, as was the case in the United Kingdom. The weaknesses in shareholder and bondholder monitoring of management inherent in public ownership, together with a policy of using proceeds to pay off government debt, led to the policy of privatization. There was heavy emphasis on deregulation of the markets in which these commercial activities operated. Deregulation was a precondition to corporatization, and was reinforced again as a condition of privatization. In a number of countries, including Australia and the United Kingdom, regulatory mechanisms have been retained in some cases to protect the shareholder value in the privatized businesses. Although there have been debates from time to time on specific issues, to date, New Zealand Governments have taken the view that their policies to promote competition overrode their fiscal interest in the value of the shares.

New Zealand's corporatization policies have almost entirely avoided placing noncommercial objectives on the businesses involved. In the few cases where noncommercial objectives have been imposed, policy requires them to be funded separately by explicit subsidy. There is no pattern of community service obligations on the businesses, as in Australia, for example. An exception is the requirement on New Zealand Post to underprice rural mail—a stipulation that came about by a rather untidy exercise of political pressure rather than as the product of a secure policy framework.

Privatization policy emphasized the maximization of the proceeds from sale by generally avoiding restrictions on ownership and being willing to sell 100 percent to a single buyer in order to gain the premium for management control of the enterprise. As a result, there are foreign owners with full control of many of the enterprises sold. There has been little effort to promote widespread shareholding by New Zealand citizens through public issues, although there was a condition on the sale of the telecommunications company that a minority stake was sold into public ownership. An earlier decision to sell a minority stake in the state's commercial bank, the Bank of New Zealand, was a failure for all parties and influenced future decisions in this regard. The share price collapsed when the bank's capital was wiped out by poor loans, and the rights of minority shareholders under company law made the reconstruction of the bank by the Government very difficult. These two features of privatization policy are distinct from the privatization policies of many other countries. A unique feature of New Zealand's privatization was the starting position, at which 12 percent of GDP was generated by businesses run from government departments.

The reforms of government departments and of other activities not fully exposed to competitive market conditions are also generally in line with the principles that underlie actual and intended reforms in a number of countries—again, most notably, the United Kingdom and some areas of Australia. In privatization policy, the United Kingdom broke new ground in many areas. In all three countries, general management principles emerge that concern the clarification of objectives, measuring and assessing performance, more effective human resource management expanding delegated authority for managing resources, introducing competition where feasible, and improving financial reporting and management. Similar principles emerge in the thinking of reformers in Canada's "Public Service 2000" initiative in 1990, and in the U.S. Vice President Gore's "National Performance Review" in 1993.

While similar in significant elements of underlying philosophy, the differences between other countries' accomplishments and New Zealand's measures become greater the more detailed is the focus on particular elements.

New Zealand's reforms covered government administration comprehensively, whereas it is more common for reforms to approach areas of government administration sequentially. This is only partially explained by the fact that reform in the United Kingdom and Australia began earlier. While there was a degree of catching up in some areas, such as aspects of financial management, two successive Governments decided to impose a wider framework that would bring immediate gains over the whole of Government. For example, unlike the United Kingdom, the management framework for New Zealand government departments covers central policy departments. The "next steps" agencies[18] in the United Kingdom concentrated on the efficiencies arising from creating systems that are similar in many respects to New Zealand's for those parts of departments that are providing services to third parties. Reform of management of the core of U.K. government administration in directions similar to New Zealand's has begun with the publication of a white paper on the employment of civil servants, and a green paper on financial management and accounting issues. Senior Whitehall civil servants will move toward employment terms similar to their New Zealand counterparts, but there will be some discre-

[18]A short account of the origins, launch, and implementation of the "Next Steps Project" in the British Civil Service (HMSO 1991). "Next Steps" is the vehicle for the delivery of the Citizen's Charter within central government via those agencies that serve the public.

tion in the hands of the Cabinet Secretary and others on some points—for example, whether all top jobs will be advertised. It is probably accurate to say that the core agencies in the United Kingdom were more vigorous in reforming the rest of government administration than the core itself. This is not uncommon internationally.

The interesting U.K. innovations of the "citizens charter"[19] and "market testing"[20] have not been formally adopted in New Zealand. This is partly because they are seen as too centralist for a system that uses performance agreements and incentives to promote concern for clients and efficient decisions about whether to "make or buy." If the incentives do not prove strong enough to overcome traditional public administration biases to be less effective in these respects, these U.K. initiatives are likely to be adopted.

In comparing New Zealand with Australia, perhaps the most significant feature is the difference regarding formal program evaluation. Australia has perhaps gone farther than any country in implementing the extensive program evaluation that has fallen out of fashion in the central government of the United States and Canada, which once championed it. U.S. and Canadian key managers comment that the evaluations were de-emphasized because they were not influential in budget decision making, so it is of interest that Australia has gone to considerable efforts to link evaluation with budgeting. In the New Zealand system, evaluation of the effectiveness of government action is, in principle, part of the fabric of the management system. The performance agreements of executives are designed to specify the results sought, and the ex post reporting and assessment processes are intended to establish whether agreed results were delivered. Whether those deliverables produced the expected outcomes, or contributed to broader strategic objectives, is a matter for policy analysis and "purchase advice" insofar as it directly affects the services delivered by government agencies. Policy analysis and review is also the activity that assesses the effectiveness of interventions other than service delivery—grants, subsidies, regulations, and institutional structures. A question that can be debated is whether, in principle, grouping all the interventions associated with a broad policy objective into a program for the purposes of budgeting and evaluation promotes the effectiveness of those processes. Adherents of program budgeting believe so, but it is hard to see why an output-based budgeting system cannot be combined with as much evaluation of the effectiveness of policy programs as required by a government. New Zealand could benefit from considerably more evaluation, but shifting from program budgeting to output budgeting has increased the emphasis on effectiveness rather than reduced it. For practical purposes, programs generally have to be identified with the budgets of single agencies. Grouping intervention costs into programs linked to broader outcomes therefore requires ad hoc rearrangements of data in some cases.

The second major difference from the Australian model is that the expenses of running New Zealand departments are allocated to the outputs required, whereas the Australian (and Canadian) approach is to group such expenses together in a category of running costs for which managers are responsible, but over which they have rather less discretion than in the New Zealand case, particularly in personnel management. Australian managers have greater discretion over their activities than their New Zealand counterparts, but more restrictions on their freedom to acquire inputs. Some states in Australia (e.g., South Australia and Tasmania) are developing management systems that are closer to the New Zealand system in terms of output-based budgeting and management. As regards financial management, Australia has clustered administrative services together—unlike New Zealand, which has left managers free to make or buy their own services provision. In New Zealand, there was an emphasis on structural reform within government departments, designed to clarify objectives, strengthen incentives for efficiency and effectiveness, and improve information flows. Structural change also played an important role in Australia and the United Kingdom but took different objectives and forms. In Australia, for example, one of the objectives was to reduce the number of government organizations, whereas the New Zealand approach has tended to break up conglomerate departments into their constituent parts, leaving a large number of divisions.

Within a different constitutional context, the reform of government in the United States has a body of underlying principles similar to New Zealand's that emerge in a number of concrete measures:

- the experiments with performance agreements for departmental heads;
- the revision of accounting standards by the Federal Accounting Standards Review Board that includes consideration of accrual accounting concepts in some areas;
- a capital charge system;

[19]The Citizen's Charter (HMSO 1991) aims to improve public services in order to respond better to the needs and wishes of customers and users; and to find more effective and efficient ways of organizing and delivering public services.

[20]Government's Guide to Market Testing (HMSO 1993). The first edition of the monthly *Market Testing Bulletin* was published in November 1993. It gives details of all work being put out to tender as part of the market testing program, enables efficient decisions about whether to make or buy.

• the Government Performance and Results Act that commits the Government to managing for outcomes in the coming years;

• the requirement that each federal agency develop a strategic plan, annual performance plans, and an ex post performance report;

• the Chief Financial Officer's Act requirement that each chief financial officer develop and maintain an integrated accounting and financial management system that provides for systematic measurement of performance;

• linking the performance plans to the President's budget; and

• the influence of the Gramm-Rudman Act and the Budget Enforcement Act on the design of New Zealand's Fiscal Responsibility Act.

Ultimately, the lack of clean lines of accountability running through the U.S. constitution's system of checks and balances adds dimensions of complexity and makes its management systems fundamentally different from New Zealand's, even though the basic ideas have much in common.

While there is much in common between the financial reforms of the core government in New Zealand and the underlying principles of financial reform adopted in some other countries, it is of interest to note some of the main features that are different about the New Zealand system:

• departments pay indirect taxes—their required rate of return on capital is benchmarked to the private sector and adjusted for taxes;

• managers' discretion over the employment conditions of staff is greater than elsewhere;

• the focus on outputs leads to *increased* detail in the Appropriation Act, whereas the trend in other countries is toward less detail;

• the Appropriation Act is based on accrual accounting;

• there is a charge for the use of capital;

• the financial statements and budget data are accrual based;

• the reform has been more comprehensive than other countries' reforms, although some individual facets of management reform have gone further in other countries; and

• the reform achieves a high degree of internal consistency by applying some simple general principles across the whole of the Government.

Several countries with governmental traditions different from those mentioned above have embarked on reforms that are similar in important respects to those cited here. Some reforms have features very similar to New Zealand's. Malaysia has embarked on a public sector management reform that has a number of features in common with the models discussed above. It is also, however, considerably different, in that Malaysia's view of its government in terms of functions and philosophical principles is also unique in many respects. The overall philosophy is captured in the following quote from a recent speech by the Chief Secretary:

> Public sector managers are now held accountable for achieving the intended outcomes of their respective programs. The focus is on results not just processes of budgetary expenditures. The reward systems of performance appraisal procedures have also been introduced as support mechanisms to ensure a higher level of motivation, discipline and delegation among public sector employees. The remuneration system introduced in 1992 will lead to flatter, less hierarchical organizations. It will also facilitate the provision of adequate recognition to excellent employees.[21]

The scheme includes the modified budgeting system that is to evolve out of traditional program-planning and budgeting by specifying outputs in terms of quality, cost, and timing, which are represented in a program agreement that establishes clear goals for departments. A microaccounting system is also to be introduced that is essentially an activity cost accounting system to track the delivery of outputs. A client's charter concept is being introduced that promotes total quality management and consultation with the public about the standards of service required. While some increased delegation is in prospect, it is unlikely to be as extensive as in New Zealand and the United Kingdom.

The Government of Singapore is introducing a financial management reform known as "budgeting for results." Singapore has been running a program-based appropriation system, but with unusual degrees of freedom to department heads to move resources between programs. Under the new system, outputs exactly parallel to the New Zealand system are to be defined for government agencies, and an activity costing system will be developed to track expenditures against budget. Singapore has also adopted concepts similar to those in U.K. agencies whereby the delegation of management discretion is conducted piecemeal. The issuance of passports by the Immigration Service is an example. Singapore has put in place an unprecedented management regime for its revenue-collecting authority, according to which the authority is rewarded on the basis of the volume of revenue it collects. Generally, however, the moves to increase financial and personnel delegation in Singapore are not intended to go as far as those in New Zealand.

Of the Latin American government reform movements, Costa Rica is perhaps the closest to New

[21]Tan Sri Dato Seri Ahmad Sarji bin Abdul Hamid, Chief Secretary to the Government, Kuala Lumpur, Malaysia, 1993.

Zealand's approach and is developing, for example, performance agreements with departmental heads.

Delegation of Management Authority

Among industrial countries, New Zealand probably has the greatest degree of authority delegation to public sector managers, but moves to increase the management freedom of public servants are becoming a global trend. The reasons that most countries resist extensive delegation of management authority are not absent in New Zealand. Concern among politicians and the media about detailed items of expenditure is just as prominent in New Zealand as elsewhere. Public accountability for expenditure has, however, passed down the line to a significant extent from ministers to civil servants. A senior public servant recently resigned over matters of personal finance and departmental expenditure. Many of the policies for line item control that were once mandated centrally have emerged as internal departmental policy, although there remains among departments significant variation consistent with the overall philosophy. The potential for oversight by the center remains. For example, the State Services Commission has audited the use of credit cards by government departments.

New Zealand has had a long tradition of "clean" government, and ministers were not particularly concerned that greater financial freedom could result in a tendency toward unethical behavior. In many countries, however, this is not the case, and some foreign observers have stated flatly that it would not be possible to risk such a system of delegation in their environment. While this is not the place for a considered examination of the question of corruption in public administration, it is observable that countries where this is considered to be a problem are also those where highly centralized systems of public administration are in place. Central controls do not stop the corruption. There are even arguments that centralization aggravates corruption, or only changes its location. In countries where corruption is a problem, there is still considerable variation in the incidence of graft among different government institutions. The major causes of corruption seem unlikely to be associated with delegation of management authority, and it would be unfortunate for countries concerned about its ethical standards to abandon the quest for more effective public administration in the belief that empowerment of managers necessarily breeds corruption.

While a number of countries are moving toward output-based management systems with accrual accounting and activity-based costing systems, few are contemplating extensive delegation of management authority. In this regard, management reforms in Singapore and Malaysia are of considerable interest.

Countries With Different Management Approaches

Asian examples of management reform are of great significance to public sector reform generally because they have elements in common with the reform movement encompassing the United Kingdom, the United States, Canada, Australia, New Zealand, and other countries, and have pioneered some developments consistent with these general philosophies. It is notable, however, that the Republic of Korea, China, and Japan are not developing in this same direction. These countries have long-established civil service traditions similar in some ways to France and Germany in that they are based on control by a close-knit, highly educated elite with enormous influence in the government system. China aside, these traditions of public administration have been associated with great economic success and offer a considerable counterweight to the managerial revolution that is passing through many other countries around the world. Notwithstanding the essential differences in core public administration, most of these countries have had clearly defined roles for the public and private sector and particularly, in the case of Japan, have undertaken a major privatization program which, as argued earlier in this report, is the biggest single initiative to improve the effectiveness of government in the British and New Zealand experience. Senior civil servants in France, Japan, the Republic of Korea, and other countries that have not been involved in managerialist developments may well have found from their tradition a powerful formula for motivating civil servants to achieve results in important areas of government administration.

A Japanese colleague sought the implications for assessment of the New Zealand and related public sector management systems of the fact that some countries have implemented highly successful programs of economic and social development with fundamentally different approaches to public sector management. Taking Japan as the outstanding example, a few brief comments can be made in response, although the question of the role of the Japanese Government in the country's development has spawned a considerable literature that is beyond the scope of this report. The Economic Development Institute of the World Bank recently published a collection of working papers[22] that explore the subject in depth, but do not lead to a single, simple conclusion on the topic. Whether Japanese economic development has been driven by the Government, the

[22]Kim Hyung-Kit, "The Japanese Civil Service and Economic Development—Lessons for Policymakers from Other Countries," Economic Development Institute of the World Bank, EDI Working Paper No. 93/43, 1993.

private sector, or some unique combination of the two is not a closed issue. It is, however, generally accepted that the Japanese civil service has played a key role in development—at least in the past, where Japanese economic policy was much more interventionist than it is today.

It is equally clear that there are other factors in place that, although in a very different political and cultural milieu, have been regarded as fundamental to successful government management in the countries referred to above. The issue is not whether Japan's economic policies have been more interventionist than those of other countries, but the characteristics of its public administration. The Japanese Government embarked on major reform in the 1980s, with both short-term objectives such as the restriction of the Government's budget, and medium-term objectives that included drastic reform of the social security system, privatization of public corporations, and the promotion of deregulation (see Ito 1993, p. 7). The Japanese Government had, in the eyes of another researcher, "managed to keep its public sector fairly small—indeed it is much smaller than its counterparts in the industrial countries—with virtually no market presence; yet it has remained a pervasive market player. It has succeeded in this endeavor by emphasizing fiscal balance and macroeconomic stability, and by avoiding misdirecting resources away from productive investment by the private sector to unproductive government consumption."[23]

The Japanese civil service has emphasized the creation of an elite, highly educated, and motivated core of senior civil servants, and also has habits and institutions of coordination in the pursuit of wider policy objectives, notwithstanding ferocious interdepartmental rivalries. As this report stressed, top-quality people who are motivated to perform and coherent strategic policy formulation are a necessary—and possibly even sufficient—condition for effective public sector management. It is an open question whether the adoption of more explicit objectives for public administration, and a more transparent financial management system, might add further to the effectiveness of the Japanese public sector. There is no reason in principle why such a management system would cause Japan's public sector efficiency to deteriorate.

Germany provides another interesting frame of reference for New Zealand's and other countries' systems based on similar philosophies. Hall (1993, p. 11) notes the closer resemblance of Germany, among European countries, to Japan. Comments similar to those above about Japan would seem reasonable.

[23]Kim Hyung-Kit (1993, p. 26).

Interdependencies Between Components of the System

It is commonly asked whether it is necessary to turn the traditional bureaucratic model of public administration inside out to achieve greater strategic coherence, client consciousness, managerial efficiency, and to make a large contribution to fiscal policy. Can some features of the New Zealand system be useful additions to a more traditional approach to public sector management? The answer is that some modules of the New Zealand system can fit comfortably within an approach to government management that is different in significant respects. Whether such a combination adds to the overall performance of the system in question naturally depends on the features of that system and the problems that a government is trying to address in changing it. In other circumstances, adopting some aspects of the New Zealand framework might be harmless but ineffective or, at worst, expensive and dysfunctional. It depends entirely on the detailed circumstances of the reforming country, and, while little can be said at a general level, a point can be made and illustrated with examples.

Countries around the world that are reforming their systems of public administration typically set objectives for cheaper and more effective service delivery, changing the role of government in some respects, encouraging greater quality and innovation in the production of public services, and exerting better fiscal control. This quest for more effective management, although highly individualized in each country's circumstances, does adhere to some generally accepted principles of effective management about which there is a large measure of agreement. The key elements of effective management are

- Strategic vision
- Clear objectives and business plans
- Resources allocated to meet objectives
- Incentives to produce results
- Freedom to manage
- Enabling management systems
- High-quality information for management and accountability
- Effective communication, and
- Values congruent with organizational mission.

Achieving greater effectiveness is not a static process, although evidence shows there are substantial short-term, one-off efficiency gains to be gleaned from introducing a program of public sector management reform. The more important objective for the longer term is to create a culture of constant improvement and innovation in service design, client consciousness, and efficiency in production and delivery. These dynamics of perpetual incremental improvement are hard to achieve and owe more to the softer elements of management concerning leadership, motivation, organizational values, and culture than to the systems, structures, and strategies that have been emphasized in this report.

Much experience in both public and private sectors points to the necessity for the components of a management system to reinforce each other in operation if a cycle of self-sustaining improvement is to be achieved. For example, performance problems can arise from lack of integration between strategic planning and operational management, between espoused values and personnel management practices, and between stated business goals and measurement systems. The components also should be integrated in a technical sense; for example, the remuneration system should reflect the results of the performance assessment system. The entire system should also be integrated in terms of the underlying values and the culture they support through the organization. It is all too common for organizations, both public and private, to draw up a statement of the values and commitments of the organization that are not reflected in either the actual behavior of managers or the operation of the management systems. It is much more important that the system as a whole functions to achieve improved performance over time than if any given component of the system can be benchmarked as best practice in some static sense. A significant defect in one component of the system can be sufficient to undermine the contribution of all other components. Such considerations form the background against which to decide whether various components of the New Zealand system might be a useful adaptation to the management systems of other countries.

The short answer is that the New Zealand system will be applicable if it removes a significant defect in the dynamic operation of the existing management system and/or is in harmony with the other elements of that system. The reverse is also true. If, for example, a country has already made a commitment to a results-based management system that explicitly specifies the objectives of a government entity, the adoption of an accrual accounting system and the application of modern cost accounting principles will improve a government's ability to assess the costs of achieving those objectives. On the other hand, the expense of installing modern management accounting systems is hard to justify in an environment where performance objectives are not properly specified. It might still be worthwhile, however, to adopt some of the generally accepted accounting principles in order to develop a consolidated balance sheet for the government entity as a whole to identify contingent liabilities and movements in the Crown's overall net worth, even though this is not part of a system of active financial management at the suborganizational level.

It is common for governments to have program-based appropriation structures that record all the expenditures incurred in the pursuit of some broad policy goal. While this has the advantage of recording information in such a way that the Government's total effort in relation to a significant objective is collected in one place, it is typical for the items within the program to be the responsibility of a range of different people in the system. No one person is accountable for the program as a whole, as discussed earlier. An output-based appropriation system could be merged with a program-based system so that all the output purchases, grants, and other appropriations associated with the broad policy area are listed together. The accountability for an output production can be clear as in the New Zealand model, while the information is drawn together in a way that facilitates debate about the wider policy area into which the outputs fit.

Many possible permutations and combinations of pieces of the New Zealand model exist with alternative approaches that depend entirely on the circumstances of the reforming country. A general principle should, however, be observed in considering any such permutations, as the following paragraphs elaborate.

Balancing Freedom and Accountability

While there are a number of ways in which imbalances in the design of the management system can cause dysfunction, the greatest concern in countries considering the implementation of modern public sector management principles relates to the consequences of an imbalance between freedom and accountability. The traditional bureaucratic model has little freedom and less accountability. It rewards compliance and creates incentives to avoid risk. While, in the writer's view, such a system is incompatible with a quest for improved performance, it has long been an extraordinarily successful and durable model of public administration. Public administrators around the world seek greater freedom but they are less anxious to seek greater accountability. It is common for visitors to New Zealand to remark that they would be concerned to see such freedoms given to public administrators in their own environment because "there would be a loss of control." Central agencies and their ministers worry that giving managerial freedom to public servants means that important leverage will be lost. The experience in New Zealand, at least insofar as fiscal policy is concerned, is that the Treasury and the Minister of Finance gave away detailed control of the financial management of government departments, but in doing so exchanged the appearance of control for the substance of control. It was, in effect, not possible under the previous system to impose restrictions on the total resource use of a government agency. It was possible, however, to insist that, for instance, staff forgo travel by taxi to an airport if a bus service was available. The new system gave away control of small numbers in exchange for control of large numbers. The reason for this fundamental trade-off is that it is not possible to limit the total amount of resources available to a public sector manager to produce a specified set of results without also extending the freedom to manage resources in order to stay within that limit. Detailed controls over management indicate the management argument that the cost of producing the specified results is not within management control and must be passed on to head office.

A system that extends freedom to managers without strengthening their accountability is inferior to both the traditional, bureaucratic model of management reform and the empowerment model exemplified by New Zealand and several other countries. No political system would tolerate the results of an inferior system for long. At each step in the evolution from centralism to decentralism, there should be a balance between the freedom granted and the accountability imposed. The approach to reform can be thought of as a ladder in which each step balances freedom and accountability and maintains the functionality of a management system. Any step that involves imbalance between freedom and accountability is dysfunctional. The system will not work if officials are held to account for events outside their control, or if they are given freedom without clear expectations of performance. While there is room for considerable variation in detail, the evolution from a system built for compliance to one designed for performance improvement can be seen as steps on the reform ladder. With each step further up the ladder, performance objectives and performance monitoring are enhanced, greater managerial freedoms are granted, competition among providers increases, and purchase interest supplants ownership interest as the channel of control. At the top rung is a hypothetical model of government administration in which only functions involving complex accountability to politicians are retained in government ownership.

Accrual Accounting

Accrual accounting is emerging as a solid trend in financial management in many countries around the world, although it is more commonly applied on a piecemeal basis than comprehensively. The state of New South Wales in Australia has had an accrual-based system for some years, and other states are following suit. The Australian federal Government is moving toward the adoption of accrual accounting. A green (discussion) paper recently issued in the United Kingdom foreshadows financial management reforms, including accrual accounting, which are similar in concept to those in New Zealand. Accrual accounting has long been accepted by many in the United States federal administration as a desirable accounting standard, but the complex relationships between the administration and Congress have led the Office of Management and Budget to resist the concept—reportedly out of concern that control would be lost in the complex accountability relationships inherent in the U.S. constitution. This is a valid point in the sense that the adoption of generally accepted accounting principles in government presumes a facility to impose strict compliance with good accounting practice, which is much easier in the simple constitutional environment of New Zealand.

Can Improved Performance Be Achieved Through Program Evaluation?

The main point of this question is whether emphasis on constant review of the effectiveness of government policy can bring about the same or greater improvements in effectiveness in a system that does not define administrative outputs, monitor performance, and provide freedom and incentives for efficiency. This is illustrated by earlier comments. It is the writer's belief that the two concepts can be thought of as complements rather than substitutes. The theory underlying the New Zealand management system emphasizes the quest for a solution to the agency problem in public administration, and emphasizes contractual obligations, the allocation of rights, information, and incentives. From this perspective, the question of how much program evaluation can add to the effectiveness of public administration depends on how it is set up. If program evaluation is done by outsiders who overlook skeptical managers who control vital flows of information, it will not be effective. An alternative framework with strong incentives for focusing evaluation on topics of strategic importance, creating strong incentives for high-quality analysis, and full information disclosure, while integrating it into the ongoing processes of policy formation and resource allocation could produce significant benefits. Even so, it is difficult to judge whether it will be an effective substitute for management reform in a country where that would otherwise be called for.

Concluding Remarks

The New Zealand experience of moving to a system of appropriation by output holds some lessons for other countries that may be contemplating similar reforms. New Zealand's experience has proved that a system of output appropriation provides a workable alternative to the traditional input-based system and can yield substantial advantages for both departmental management and government decision makers. There were problem areas, such as in the definition and measurement of policy advice outputs. Initial attempts at measuring the provision of policy advice did, however, assess the relative value of such outputs more effectively than was the case under the input appropriation system.

New Zealand has not yet answered all the questions that have been raised by the move to output appropriation and output costing. However, many of the practical and technical problems have been addressed and have helped to provide a functional system in their current form. The system of delegated management freedom has empowered the most talented and motivated managers to bring about organizational transformations unheard of under the traditional management system. While lesser managers have not used their greater freedom to such effect and while there have been some minor abuses, eight years of experience show that reforming the system is generally both practicable and worthwhile. Statistical evidence of detailed causal links between management reforms and the achievement of fiscal goals is hard to pin down, but what there is supports the views of ministers, who were the key decision makers at the time. They believe that the reforms to government commercial activities in the mid-1980s cleaned out inefficiencies on a massive scale with major impacts on fiscal outcomes. They also believe that the reforms to the rest of the public sector in the late 1980s provided the tools to shift priorities, to reverse the trend growth in the share of government expenditures, and to force improvements in efficiency in the production of public services.

Appendix I Outline of Treasury Instructions

The following is the table of contents from the new Treasury instructions.

Applying to departments receiving Mode B appropriations

Appendix II Summary of Aggregate Fiscal Reports

The following illustrates the annual financial cycle of the Parliament.

Proposed Annual Cycle for Select Committee Review and House Debate

Ex post review phase—Crown financial statements

By mid-October

Crown financial statements for previous financial year brought forward.

Mid-October to mid-December

Finance and Expenditure Committee (FEC) reviews Crown financial statements and reports to House of Parliament before December 25 (instead of by 31 March, as currently required by Standing Order 329(2)).

When House resumes in February/March

House debates FEC report on Crown financial statements during second reading of Appropriation (Financial Review) Bill. (The FEC debate currently takes place in April/May. Standing Order 322(1) envisages this bill being introduced before 31 March.)

Pre-budget phase—half-year economic and fiscal update and budget policy statement

December

Minister of Finance to publish half-year economic and fiscal update prepared by the Treasury.

February/March

FEC reviews half-year economic and fiscal update.

By end-March

Minister of Finance to publish budget policy statement.

By end-April

FEC reviews budget policy statement and reports to the House of Parliament on half-year economic and fiscal update and on budget policy statement.

No later than first sitting week in May

The House of Parliament debates FEC report on half-year economic and fiscal update and on budget policy statement during first Wednesday general debate after FEC report brought forward.

Budget phase—fiscal strategy report and budget economic and fiscal update

Budget night

Minister of Finance prepares a fiscal strategy report and a budget economic and fiscal update.

July to September

FEC reviews fiscal strategy report and the budget economic and fiscal update and reports to House by 30 September.

October

The House of Parliament debates FEC report on fiscal strategy and the budget economic and fiscal update during third reading of first Appropriation Bill relating to new financial year.

Source: New Zealand House of Representatives, *Parliament's Annual Financial Cycle* (Wellington, 1996).

Appendix III Schedule of Reforms Enacted Between 1984 and 1991

Factor Market

Finance

Abolition of credit growth guideline	1984
Removal of separate requirements for trustee banks, building societies, finance houses, and stockbrokers	1985–87
Removal of quantity restrictions and other entry barriers to banking	1985–86
End of formal financial controls (reserve ratio requirements, sector lending priorities)	1985
Removal of interest rate controls	1984
Abolition of export credit guarantees	1984
Removal of ownership restrictions on financial institutions	1985
Liberalization of stock exchange	1986

Energy

Corporatization of state coal mines	1987
Financial restructuring of oil refinery	1988–91
Legalization of oil company ownership of service stations	1988
End of price control (except on natural gas)	1984–88
Sale of state natural gas exploitation/distribution interests	1988–90
Sale of other state energy holdings	1990–92
Corporatization and restructuring of electricity generation, transmission, and distribution	1986–91

Transport

Removal of restrictions on road and rail carriage	1983–86
End of quantity licensing of trucking	1984
Corporatization of state rail, air, and bus services	1982–84
Tendering of local authority bus services and liberalization of licensing requirements	1990–91
Deregulation of taxi industry	1990
Opening up of domestic aviation industry	1987
Granting of number of landing and on-flying rights to foreign airlines in New Zealand	1989
Corporatization or sale of airports and Airways Corporation	1986–91
Corporatization of ports	1989
Deregulation of stevedoring industry	1990
Removal of cabotage on coastal shipping	1991

Research and Development

Removal of concessions for research and development to put on equal footing with all investment	1984
Cost recovery of public research and development work	1985
Establishment of contestable pool of public funds (Foundation of research, science, and technology)	1990
Corporatization of government research bodies (Crown research institutes)	1992

Labor Market

Introduction of voluntary unionism	1983
More market-based bargaining under Industrial Relations Act Amendment: compulsory unionism reinstituted	1984
Some contestability in union coverage under Labor Relations Act	1987
Radical reform via Employment Contracts Act (voluntary unionism, contestable unions of any size, and any arrangements for employer/employee bargaining at joint or individual level)	1990

Industry

Product Markets

Termination of supplementary minimum prices on agricultural products	1984
Agricultural tax concessions removed	1985
Termination of concessional financing of primary producer stocks held by producer boards	1986–88
Review of compulsory producer marketing board arrangements	1987
Termination of domestic boards for eggs, mills, and wheat	1984–88
Termination of export market development incentive schemes	1984
Phase out export performance tax incentives	1984–87

Industrial Regulations

End of wage/price freeze	1984
Termination of price control and replacement by (unused) price surveillance powers under Commerce Act	1984–88
Removal of quantity licensing on almost all industries, and end of quality regulation on most industries	1986–88
End of all state-regulated monopoly rights (except letter post, air traffic control, and milk distribution)	1984–86
Removal of some occupational licensing	1985–90
Removal of producer cooperative tax advantages	1989
Termination of restrictions on shop trading hours	1989

Business Law

Establishment of Commerce Act as liberal, efficiency-based regime to govern mergers and trade practices	1986
Fair Trading Act governing consumer rights	1986
Review of securities legislation and takeover law (extent of efficiency approach still under discussion)	1988–91
Review of intellectual property regime (patent, copyright, trademarks, and designs acts)	1990–91
Review of town and country planning	1987–90
Resource Management Act to govern more liberal planning and environmental legislation	1991
Crown Minerals Act to clarify property rights to mineral resources	1991

International Trade and Monetary Policy

Import Protection

Phasing out of import licensing requirements	1983–89
Reduction of import tariffs according to Swiss formula, to 10 percent from an average of 28 percent	1986–92
Additional one-third reduction in import tariffs (planned)	1992–96

Removal of special protection features for 18 specific "industry plan" sectors and incorporation into general tariff reform program	1984–92
Slower reduction of tariffs on two remaining "special" industries (motor vehicles and components; and textiles, clothing, and footwear)	1987–96

International Capital Controls

Removal of controls on external investment/borrowing	1984
Free entry of foreign direct investment (approved by New Zealand Overseas Investment Commission)	1985, 1989
Very liberal regime for portfolio investment and repatriation of profit	1985

Exchange Rate Controls

Deregulation of foreign exchange trading	1984
Twenty percent devaluation against basket of currencies	1984
Free float of currency on foreign exchange markets without direct control	1985

Monetary Policy

Devotion of monetary policy instruments to deflation, with target of price stability (0 to 2 percent price increase) by 1992–93	1989
Tight monetary policy (M3-growth held below rate of inflation)	1987 to date
Independence of Reserve Bank from the Government, formalized through Reserve Bank Act	1989

Government Sector

State Trading Operations

Removal of almost all state-regulated monopoly rights	1984–89
Corporatization of 24 state-owned enterprises (in transport, finance, tourism, forestry, broadcasting, utilities, and service industries)	1987–88
Restructuring to isolate natural monopoly elements of state-owned enterprises	1989–91
Full or partial privatization of Air New Zealand, Bank of New Zealand, Petroleum Corporation, Tourist Hotel Corporation, Shipping Corporation, Rural Bank, Government Life, Forestry Corporation, Post Office Bank, Telecom Corporation, and others	1987–91
Further privatization planned via divestment of asset sales, sale of rights, share sales, etc.	1991
Requirement for local authorities to corporatize local authority trading enterprises (LATEs) and tender out services	1990–91
Encouragement to local authorities to sell holdings in airports, port companies, and local utilities	1991
Sale of other assets, for example, irrigation schemes and fishing rights	1983–88

Taxation

Broadened tax base through Goods and Services Tax on virtually all final domestic consumption without exception (now 12.5 percent)	1986
Flattening and lowering of personal income tax rate, with top rate standardized to corporate tax levels and aimed to minimize poverty traps	1988
Standardization and simplification of corporate taxation to minimize evasion and cut administrative costs	1985
Removal of most other indirect taxes	1986–91
Removal of tax concessions for savings, etc., to put on neutral footing	1987

Expenditure Control

Attempts at reduction in government expenditure, especially in areas of administration and industry development	1985 to date
Assignment of proceeds of sale of state-owned enterprise assets to repay public debt	1987 to date
Public sector management reform through Public Finance Act	1989
Reform of core government departments on corporate lines through State Sector Act of 1988, with separation of policy, provision, and funding	1986 to date
User-pays principles for remaining state trading activity	1986 to date
Redesign of government accounts on more commercial basis, accrual accounting, and output-based monitoring systems through Public Finance Act	1988
Abolition of 50 quasi-nongovernmental and quasi-governmental organizations	1987
Renewed attempt at reduction in social spending (education, health, social welfare, and superannuation)	1991

Social Services

Reforms of compulsory education system, based on elected boards of trustees	1988–90
Quasi-corporatization and fee-paying for tertiary education institutions	1992
Integration of state housing assistance into private sector rental and mortgage provision	1991
Tightening of requirements and reduction of levels of unemployment benefits and other government social transfers	1990
Tightening of requirements, extension of age, and reduction of benefits for government-funded old-age pension scheme	1989–91
Separation of funding from provision of state health services, establishment of Crown health enterprises, and expectations of private sector crowd-in	1992
Likely development of private funding arrangements for health provision	1992

Source: Alan Bollard and Ian Duncan, 1992, *Corporatization & Privatization—Lessons from New Zealand* (Oxford: Oxford University Press).

Appendix IV Ministry of Defence: Contingent Military Capabilities

The question of what outputs the military is producing has no simple answer, and extensive debates were held before reaching an acceptable approach. Conceptually, the desired outputs should be derived from the country's strategic objectives for its defense and international relations. There is a respectable argument that the best solution is through organizational separation and an arm's-length relationship between the purchase and delivery functions. This was put into practice in New Zealand when the Ministry of Defence was given control of the purchase of equipment for the New Zealand Defence Force. Practical problems, such as the ability of the small ministry to obtain information and develop the necessary practical expertise, led to a degree of reintegration known as the "diarchy" in which the roles of the Secretary of Defence and the Chief of Defence Force overlap. Also, the small size of the Force has the consequence that large items of equipment, such as warships, are used for joint production of numerous outputs in the pursuit of multiple strategic objectives simultaneously. This creates great difficulties for cost accountants in defining outputs that can be costed accurately and separately funded. The current thinking is that outputs for which appropriations are provided are capabilities, which means that the ability to deploy a specific force is to be maintained at a specified readiness.

These efforts to apply more rational management to the military are considered worthwhile. The Chief of the Defence became enthusiastic about the vastly improved management information available to him for running the military, and these improvements greatly facilitated the management of substantial cuts in defense funding at the time. The information reported to Parliament about the New Zealand Defence Force increased from 6 pages of uninformative input costs for the Army, Navy, and Air Force to 60 pages of information regarding capabilities, objectives, and their associated costs.

The following is an excerpt from the *Estimates of Appropriations for the Government of New Zealand for the year ended 30 June 1995* (Part I, p. 237), providing maritime information.

Contingent Capability to Provide Maritime Surveillance and Presence Operations

Description

Output Class 1 comprises the capability to conduct maritime surveillance and maintain a naval presence in a low-threat environment. Table 7 illustrates the costs associated with Output Class 1.

This class also provides the minimum level from which a capability can be generated to conduct the same operations, with allied forces, in conflict up to mid-level. The main tasks would be monitoring maritime activities; deterring intrusions; demonstrating rights of innocent passage; or contributing to a blockade, e.g., to enforce sanctions.

The frigates, Wasp helicopters, and fleet tankers of the Naval Combat Force, and the Orion aircraft of the Long-Range Maritime Patrol Force, conduct essential training and assigned tasks, within their annual appropriations, to achieve defined levels of preparedness.

Quantity, Quality, and Cost of Maritime Surveillance and Presence Operations

- The Frigate Force will conduct 150 sea days of surveillance and presence operations, which will include readiness training activities to generate and maintain the minimum level of capability for such operations.

Table 7. Cost: Output Class 1

	$ millions
Personnel	6,536
Operating	4,978
Depreciation	4,244
Capital charge	4,719
Total expenses	20,477
Other revenue	—
Crown revenue	20,477
	(Goods and services tax exclusive)

Source: *Estimates of Appropriations for the Government of New Zealand for the year ended 30 June 1995*, Part I, p. 237.

• Wasp helicopters of each Frigate will conduct a total of 120 hours of readiness training in detecting and identifying contacts, and transporting boarding parties during surveillance or presence operations.

• The level of capability generated by each Frigate and its helicopter will be measured by their performance in exercises such as TASMANEX, KAKADU, Fleet Concentration Period 94/2, or Fleet Training Period 95 during the Aggregate Reporting Period for each ship.

• The fleet tanker will conduct readiness training in replenishing frigates at sea while on deployment and on surveillance patrols. Procedures will be evaluated during exercises TASMANEX and STARFISH, or Fleet Concentration Period 94/2.

• The Long Range Maritime Patrol Force will conduct 30 hours of maritime search and readiness training (detecting, monitoring, and reporting procedures) to generate and maintain the minimum level of capability in maritime surveillance operations.

• The level of proficiency of each operationally qualified crew on No. 5 Squadron in maritime surveillance procedures will be assessed during exercises TASMANEX 95, STARFISH 94, and FCP 94/2, routine surveillance patrols and oceanic search and rescue missions.

Appendix V Evolution of New Zealand's Health Policies

Historical Developments

New Zealand's health system was previously based on that of the U.K. system, with public universal funding and little or no charges at the point of use. There was a mix of public and private sector providers. Doctors worked in hospitals on salaries but also ran private practices on the side.

The system was converted from national to regional in the 1980s through the establishment of area health boards with local political representation at first, and government appointments added later.[24] Parliament appropriated funds under "vote health" to these boards with restrictions on who could benefit—essentially directing funds to hospitals the boards owned. General medical practitioners were paid by the "general medical services" benefit, which became constrained, thereby increasing the patient share of doctors' fees.

This created incentives for purchase of private supplementary health insurance or for going to the "free" hospital rather than to the expensive doctor. Hence, resources were being channeled to expensive hospital care when primary care by other means was less costly. Policymakers saw the need for integration of funding primary and secondary care, which required a neutral purchaser.

After the Public Finance Act was passed in 1989, its principles were applied so that area health boards had contracts with the Minister of Health specifying outcomes, outputs, budget, performance indicators, and reporting requirements.[25]

The 1993 Health Reforms

What Was Intended

In 1991, reforms were announced and published in *Your Health and the Public Health*, a green and white paper. Its basic features were:[26]

(1) Integration of funding of primary and secondary care, as well as some attempts to integrate funding coming through the Accident Compensation Corporation (ACC) and continuing care (rest homes, etc.).

(2) Separation of purchasing care and providing care through the establishment of four regional health authorities (RHAs) to act as purchasers of health care.

(3) Abolition of the 14 area health boards and reorganization of public hospitals into Crown health enterprises (CHEs) operating with commercial objectives and also community trusts as owners of some local hospitals.

(4) Public health services to be purchased and coordinated by the centralized Public Health Commission (which was abolished in 1994, and its functions given back to the Ministry of Health and attached to regional health authorities in 1995).

(5) Individuals would have the opportunity to opt out of their regional health authority and choose an alternative health care plan (HCP) as their purchasing agency. They would take an entitlement of government funding to the health care plan that was related to their health profile.

(6) A national advisory committee on core health services would be established to advise the Minister of Health on what personal health services should be provided on a reasonably accessible and affordable basis to all New Zealanders.

(7) Introduction of a regime to target user charges for health services and the introduction of the kiwi card (later renamed a community services card).

At the same time, user charges were raised in a regime that targeted assistance to low-income groups by classifying every person into one of three groups. Service "stop-loss" provisions established a maximum number of prescriptions and charges for service on a family basis, after which additional costs were fully or partly paid by the Government, depending on the family's income. The '"high-use health card" was established so that people who required service more than six times within six months paid no fees for hospital service and received reduced charges for prescriptions and an increased general practitioner (GP) subsidy (Figure 4).

---

[24]Loraine Hawkins, "Purchasing Health Services," *Public Sector*, March 1995.

[25]Organization for Economic Cooperation and Development, *The Reform of Health Care Systems: A Review of Seventeen OECD Countries* (Paris: OECD), pp. 229–31, 1994.

[26]Claudia D. Scott, "Reform of the New Zealand Health Care System," *Health Policy*, pp. 25–40, 1994.

Figure 4. Proposed Health Care Structures (1991)

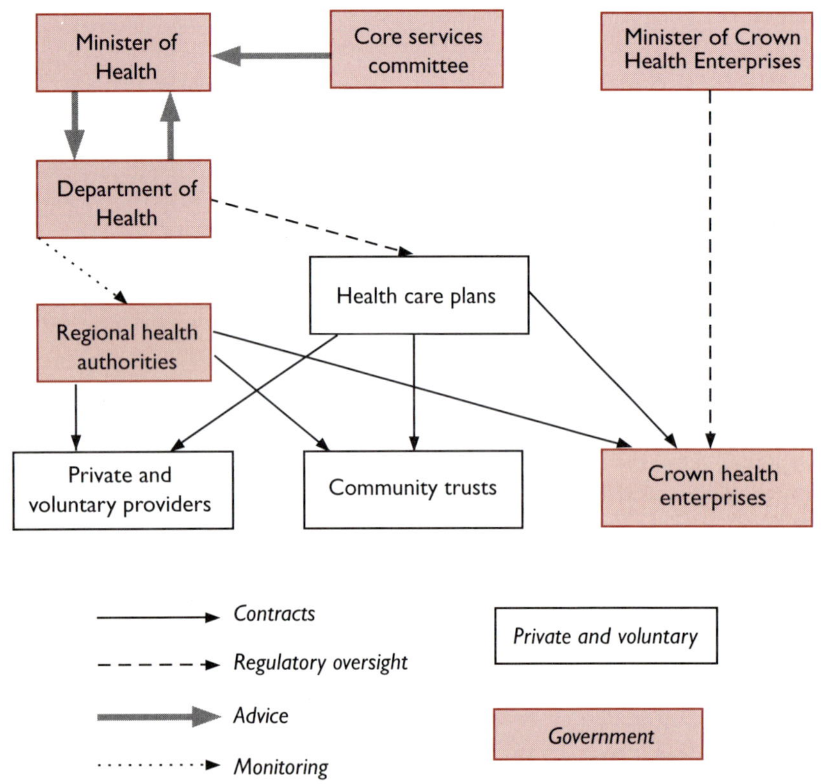

Source: Claudia D. Scott, "Reform of the New Zealand Health Care System," *Health Policy*, Vol. 29, Nos. 1 and 2 (August 1994), pp. 25–40.

Note the influence of ideas underlining the rest of the public sector reforms. The purchaser/provider split distinguishes the Government's interests as owner and purchaser. Crown health enterprises are modeled after state-owned enterprises.

What Was Done

Crown health enterprises' commercial objectives were modified to require them to meet the following list of health objectives and to "be as successful and efficient as comparable businesses not owned by the Crown."

(1) Like all state-owned enterprises, they are required to exhibit a sense of social responsibility. Requirements on them for open access also contributed to a general pattern of non-neutrality between Crown health enterprises and private providers.

(2) The extension of copayments for hospital services was unpopular and watered down.

(3) Disability support services were added to the responsibilities of regional health authorities, but with the activity separately accounted for and funded by the ACC. As a consequence, the core services committee brief was expanded to cover disability services.

(4) Provision for health care plans in the legislation has been overridden by the Government's announcement that it has no present plans to progress these. (The Minister of Health's approval is required.) The reforms were a two-stage plan moving from purchaser-provider splits to competitive purchasers (health care plans), but the difficulties with the first made the second a nonstarter, with political difficulties regarding reforms as a whole. Allowing people to opt out requires income-testing and risk-

Figure 5. Advisory and Contracting Relationships in the Health Care System (1993)

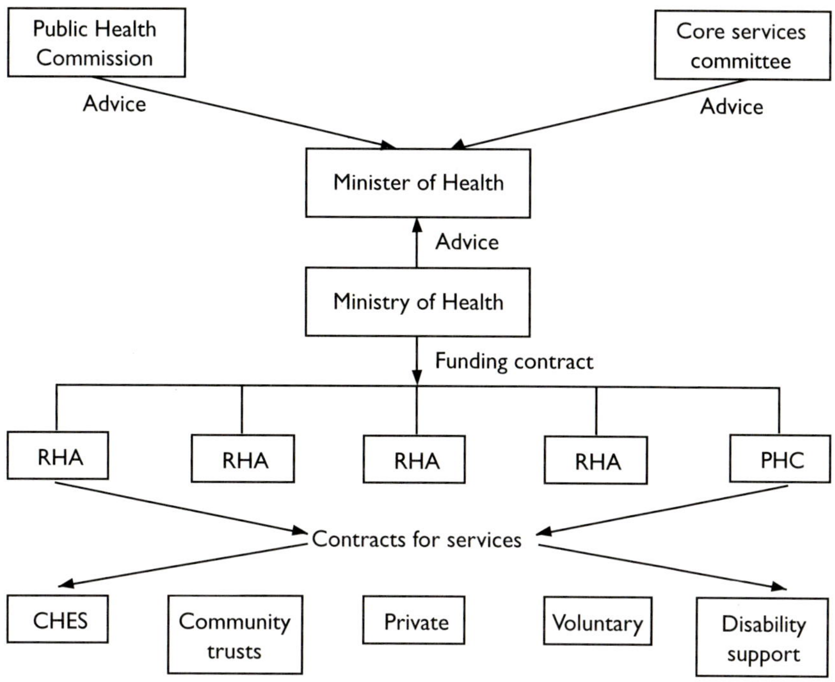

Source: Claudia D. Scott, "Reform of the New Zealand Health Care System," *Health Policy*, Vol. 29, Nos. 1 and 2 (August 1994), pp. 25–40.

rating. Experts questioned the ability to risk rate, and Maori groups wanted to establish health care plans, but their health status is poorer than the population as a whole, raising doubts about the financial viability of Maori health care plans. Also, insurers showed no interest, since they were concerned with setting up hospitals, not insurance companies.

(5) The comprehensive targeting regime published in 1991 a pamphlet entitled "Social Assistance Welfare That Works," which was later abandoned. "Welfare That Works" conformed to principles laid down in the economic and social initiative of 1990. It amalgamated all benefits into a comprehensive plan that targeted family income, giving each family a credit card and an account number that put ceilings on the family's expenditures on charges and fees. It envisaged a premium-based funding system, with the Government targeting low-income and high-use families. Instead, only charges for some outpatients in the highest of the three income groups were retained. The prospect of bringing much more private funds into the system was lost because the public was not involved from the outset as to what the problem was and how to solve it. The debate as to whether the system should be universal or targeted still continues today (Figure 5).

Transitional Issues

Regional health authorities were instructed by the Government to take the following measures:

(1) Allocate funds on the same basis as during the first year (the 1993/94 financial year).

(2) Allocate much more funds than envisaged to Crown health enterprises to keep them more financially viable.

(3) "Grandfather" disability services so that the income qualification did not apply to those already in medical care for several years.

(4) Retain a fee for service payments to GPs and private specialists. Hence, there is still open-ended funding—though progress is being made by establishing contracts with providers, including groups of GPs known as independent practice associations (IPAs).

Evaluation of the Current System

Efficiency

There has been substantial funding of primary and secondary health care. Choice and competition have been significantly enhanced. There is good potential for shifting resources across services and service providers. Contracts with some independent practice associations have made significant gains in the management of pharmaceutical budgets. There is more information than ever about health entitlements and costs.

Expenditure Control

There has been a reduction in open-ended funding arrangements with fixed budgets for regional health authorities, a growth in fixed budget arrangements in primary care with independent practice associations, and price-volume contracting for hospital services.

Crown health enterprises sometimes take direct political action to bypass regional health authorities and resort to government lending. Doctors and the media at some point have put pressure to reverse decisions to withhold treatment. Crown health enterprises sometimes go public about their queues and try to blame the Government or regional health authorities for their problems.

Cumming (1994, p. 55)[27] argues that the objectives for a comprehensive core service and limiting expenditure appear contradictory. (Most countries have free access to primary care.) If there is to be expenditure restraint, then the design should focus on trade-offs between cost to the Government and efficiency. Ideally, we should compare relative efficiency and equity of private and public insuring arrangements.

Equity

The equity goal is to provide all citizens with reasonable access to core health services according to health needs. The emphasis is on access rather than outcome.

Targeting is intended to focus limited resources on those with poor health and low income. Clarification and uniformity of public entitlements are to be improved.

Access is, however, also related to cultural barriers and other social factors that go beyond ability to pay and service availability. Maori health indicators, though improving, are consistently lower than the population as a whole.

The Maori were particularly interested in health care plans offering empowerment and control over health resources.

Core Services Definition

Overhanging the whole reform is the relative failure of the core service concept. There are problems with the use of medical procedures as the focus, when the appropriateness of any procedure depends on the circumstances and the attributes of the person receiving the care. The focus should be on the effectiveness of interventions from a research base. It should also be conceived within a budget constraint if the notion of the core is to be useful to purchasers and providers. The Core Services Committee advises the Minister of Health, and the committee's recommendations are not binding but perceived as public participation rather than a key link in the system.

Issues for the Future

Who Decides What Is To Be Purchased?

Ultimately, Parliament decides what is to be purchased through a minister who delegates to purchasers. What are the possible implications of the indifferent record of the attempt to define a core of services available to all? Was it a good concept (based on the state of Oregon in the United States) that was poorly developed? Can the core be redefined to harmonize with a budget-constrained system and not be a guaranteed list of rights to service regardless of cost?

Is the Purchaser-Provider Split Working?

There are useful technical solutions to the problems of specifying output and effectiveness. The diagnostic related group (DRG) concept is being refined rapidly and is working well. Few attempts have been made to standardize the effectiveness of treatments using, for example, quality-adjusted life years. Care will be needed to avoid defining services in such a way that innovation is discouraged through excessively detailed or historical descriptions.

---

[27] Jacqueline Cumming, "Core Services and Priority-setting: The New Zealand Experience," *Health Policy*, pp. 41–60, 1994.

The split presumes that contracts can be written and successfully monitored, and that this is superior to an integrated management approach in which the providers work for the "purchasers" in an employment relationship. The conceptual question to be asked is which structure controls the agency and public choice problems best. While the split has produced the benefits noted above, the incentives and pressures for effective contracts have been muted by transitional restrictions on moving resources around and a lack of contestability in providing many services. For much of the service, there is only one effective provider so the contract is between a monopoly purchaser and a monopoly provider. The original design envisaged more competitive pressure on both sides of the contract: health care plans in the purchase area and more competition between private and public providers of services than has occurred. Economic theory says that contracting between monopolists is always a problem, as the outcome is not driven by the underlying opportunity costs.

Also, in the background, the Government is funder, purchaser, and owner of the providing institutions, which gives it an inherent conflict that is difficult to manage but has been successfully done.

Contracting difficulties may be driven in part by the lack of competitive pressure on parties to get it right and conflicts of interest in doing so. However, we cannot know if this is true, except by experimentation, and there is no international experience that proves that this is easy to do. This suggests that the path of wisdom is to focus on improved contracting as a priority and steadily increase the contestability as confidence in contracting grows. There appear to be large potential benefits to service and efficiency from developing more complex longer-term contracts in some ways similar to models found in the private sector, where purchasers are heavily dependent on the performance of suppliers. If it becomes clear that the contracting problems are inferior to the problems of running a more integrated system, then it would be time to rethink the policy. In fact, the policy is evolving at the margin today by constant rebalancing of the roles of central coordination by the Ministry of Health and the delegated purchasing functions of the regional health authorities.

The conundrum is that the split has great merit, in part because of the monopoly situation of purchasers and providers. For example, in the U.S. health system, purchasing and providing are being linked together in health maintenance organizations (HMOs) and managed care plans as a competitive market response. If purchasers are eventually put under competitive pressure, as was originally planned, then the same market forces would in time determine whether the split is the most efficient response to inherent agency cost problems.

Conclusion

New Zealand's health reforms have been dominated by debates about structure and ideology battles over the "Americanization" of the health system.

Establishing the Crown health enterprises as businesses at first exposed that they were largely bankrupt. The managerial reforms have brought many outsiders into the health system and created much friction as cultures have been changed. As in other areas of public sector reform, one would expect to see people with both managerial ability and a strong sector background in positions of responsibility. We have conflicts between medical professionals, managers, and the Government over who should control the system.

In the absence of a defined core service that takes into account budget constraints, contracts will have to be evolved that allow for the reality that it is medical professionals who finally decide what interventions to make.

Smart purchasing is relatively new and may evolve into complex relational contracts that look increasingly like employment contracts in areas where service performance standards are hard to define. There are specific investments and high levels of uncertainty.

As long as the Government remains the people's agent in purchasing health services, it will be concerned with total expenditure on health and will attempt to impose budget constraints by any means. While the Government restricts competition and monopolizes service provision, its fiscal concerns will be reflected in the share of GDP spent on health services. In a conventional market environment, this spending would be of no public policy concern, but when the Government takes such heavy responsibilities on itself, it must be directly concerned with efficiency and equity issues in the purchaser and provider markets. It remains an open question in political debate in New Zealand as to whether the Government's overall policy framework and, in particular, the structural separations in place are the best way to achieve these objectives.

An evolutionary approach in which contracting becomes more effective, even if more complex, and greater contestability is introduced on the provider side initially and the purchaser side later, makes sense.

Bibliography

Accountants' Journal (special issue), 1992, "New Zealand Public Sector Reform" (June).

Ball, I.,1990, "Changes in Accounting and Auditing Practices: The New Zealand Experience," in *Budgetary Management and Control,* ed. by J. Foster and J. Wanna (Melbourne).

_____, 1993, "Accrual Accounting in the Public Sector: The New Zealand Experience," presented to the Institute for International Research (IIR) Conference, Canberra, Australia, April 5–6, 1993.

Boston, J., J. Martin, J. Pallot, and P. Walsh, eds., 1991, *Reshaping the State: New Zealand's Bureaucratic Revolution* (Auckland: Oxford University Press).

Cameron, R.L., and P.J. Duignan, 1984, "Government-Owned Enterprises: Theory, Performance, and Efficiency," paper presented to the New Zealand Association of Economists Conference in Wellington (February).

Controller and Auditor General of New Zealand, 1989, "Central Government Management," and 1990, "Performance Reporting in the Public Sector," Wellington, New Zealand.

de Boer, David, and Lewis Evans, 1994, "Government Department to Public Corporation in a Deregulated Economy: The Economic Efficiency of New Zealand Telecommunications," Wellington, New Zealand.

Douglas, R., and L. Callan, 1992, *Towards Prosperity. People and Politics in the 1980s: A Personal View* (Auckland: David Bateman Ltd.).

Duncan, Ian, and Alan Bollard, 1992, *Corporatization and Privatization—Lessons from New Zealand* (Auckland: Oxford University Press).

Gibbs, Darren, 1995, "Potential Output: Concepts and Measurement," in *Labour Market Bulletin. A Journal of New Zealand Labour Market Research* (New Zealand Department of Labour), pp. 72–115.

Goldman, F., and E. Brashares, 1991, "Performance and Accountability: Budget Reform in New Zealand," *Public Budgeting & Finance* (Winter), pp. 75–85.

Hall, Peter A., 1993, "The Japanese Civil Service and Economic Development in Comparative Perspective," Economic Development Institute Working Paper No. 93/42 (Washington: World Bank).

Hawke, G.R., ed., 1993, *Improving Policy Advice*, Institute of Policy Studies (Wellington: Victoria University).

Heskett, James L., W. Earl Sasser, Jr., and Christopher W.L. Hart, 1990, *Service Breakthroughs—Changing the Rules of the Game* (New York: The Free Press).

Heymann, David B., 1988, "Input Controls in the Public Sector: What Does Economic Theory Offer?" IMF Working Paper 88/59 (Washington: International Monetary Fund).

Horn, Murray J., 1995, *The Political Economy of Public Administration—Institutional Choice in the Public Sector* (Cambridge: Cambridge University Press).

Hyung-Ki, Kim, 1993, "The Japanese Civil Service and Economic Development—Lessons for Policymakers from Other Countries," Economic Development Institute Working Paper No. 93/43 (Washington: World Bank).

Ito, Mitsutoshi, 1993, "Administrative Reform," Economic Development Institute Working Paper No. 93/33 (Washington: World Bank).

James, C., 1992, *New Territory: The Transformation of New Zealand: 1984–92* (Wellington: Bridget Williams).

Luxton, John, The Honorable, Minister of Housing, 1991, "Housing Accommodation—Accommodation Assistance" (Wellington).

Martin, J., 1992, "Transformation of a Bureaucracy: The New Zealand Experience," a paper prepared for the Commonwealth Secretariat Management Development Program (Wellington).

Ministerial Science Taskgroup, 1991, Crown Research Institute Research Companies for New Zealand (Wellington).

Ministry of Education, 1988, *Report of Education Administration in New Zealand* (Wellington).

Ministry of Transport, *"Tirohanga Tomua"—Insights on Change: Organizational Change in the Ministry of Transport 1987–92* (Wellington).

_____, 1993, *Transport in New Zealand* (Wellington).

Nethercote, J.R., Brian Galligan, and Cliff Walsh, eds., 1993, *Decision Making in New Zealand Government* (Canberra: Federalism Research Center, The Australian National University).

Organization for Economic Cooperation and Development, 1988, 1990, and 1993, *OECD Economic Surveys* (Wellington).

Palmer, Honorable Sir Geoffrey, *Memorandum to Graham Scott Dated July 21, 1994* (Wellington).

Report of the Controller and Auditor-General, 1978, "Financial Management and Control in Administrative Government Departments" (Wellington: Government Printer).

Science and Technology Advisory Committee, 1988, "New Zealand Science and Technology New Deal" (Wellington).

Scott, Claudia D., 1992, "Public Policy, Policy Analysis and Health Sector Reform," Inaugural Address, August 21, 1991, Victoria University Press.

_____, 1992, *Public Sector,* Vol. 15 (June), pp. 19–24.

Scott, Graham, 1993, *Reflections about the New Zealand Budgetary Process: Decision Making in New Zealand Government* (Canberra: Federalism Research Centre, The Australian National University), pp. 116–124.

_____, 1995, "Improving Fiscal Responsibility," *Agenda,* Vol. 2, No. 1 (Victoria, Australia).

Scott, G., and P. Gorringe, 1989, "Reform of the Core Public Sector: The New Zealand Experience," *Australian Journal of Public Administration* (March), pp. 81–92.

Scott, Graham and Lockwood Smith, the Honorable, Minister of Education, 1991, "Education Policy—Investing in People, Our Greatest Asset" (Wellington).

Scott, G., P. Bushnell, and N. Sallee, 1990, "Reform of the Core Public Sector: The New Zealand Experience," *Governance* (April), pp. 138–167.

Spicer, B.H., 1993, "Conceptual Issues of Costing and Cost Management in New Zealand's Public Sector Organizations," *Pacific Accounting Review*, Vol. 5, No. 1 (Wellington).

State Services Commission of New Zealand, 1988, *Administering Top Management and Reviewing Performance*, International Conference on Civil Service Change (Ottawa).

_____, 1990, *Changing the Public Service Culture, A Radical Approach.*

_____, 1991, *A Guide to the Employment Contracts Act.*

_____, 1991, *Review of the Purchase of Policy Advice from Government Departments* (December).

_____, 1992, *Chief Executive Performance Agreement, Guidelines and Pro Forma* (May).

_____, 1992, *Chief Executive Performance Management, Information for Ministers* (May).

Taskforce for the Review of Education Administration, Picot report, 1988, *Administering for Excellence.*

The Audit Office, 1993, "Cost Allocation Systems," *Report of the Controller and Auditor-General, Second Report for 1993.*

The New Zealand Treasury, *Briefings to the Incoming Government: Economic Management, 1984; Government Management, 1987, 1990, and 1993.*

_____, 1989, *Financial Management Policy Papers* (December).

_____, 1990, *Putting it Simply: An Explanatory Guide to Financial Management Reform.*

_____, 1994, *Improving Output Costing—Guidelines and Examples* (April).

_____, *Guidelines for 1994/95 Purchase Agreements.*

Upton, Simon, The Honorable, Minister of Health, 1991, "Health Policy—Your Health and the Public Health Summary" (Wellington).

Recent Occasional Papers of the International Monetary Fund

140. Government Reform in New Zealand, by Graham C. Scott. 1996.

139. Reinvigorating Growth in Developing Countries: Lessons from Adjustment Policies in Eight Economies, by David Goldsbrough, Sharmini Coorey, Louis Dicks-Mireaux, Balazs Horvath, Kalpana Kochhar, Mauro Mecagni, Erik Offerdal, and Jianping Zhou. 1996.

138. Aftermath of the CFA Franc Devaluation, by Jean A.P. Clément, with Johannes Mueller, Stéphane Cossé, and Jean Le Dem. 1996.

137. The Lao People's Democratic Republic: Systemic Transformation and Adjustment, edited by Ichiro Otani and Chi Do Pham. 1996.

136. Jordan: Strategy for Adjustment and Growth, edited by Edouard Maciejewski and Ahsan Mansur. 1996.

135. Vietnam: Transition to a Market Economy, by John R. Dodsworth, Erich Spitäller, Michael Braulke, Keon Hyok Lee, Kenneth Miranda, Christian Mulder, Hisanobu Shishido, and Krishna Srinivasan. 1996.

134. India: Economic Reform and Growth, by Ajai Chopra, Charles Collyns, Richard Hemming, and Karen Parker with Woosik Chu and Oliver Fratzscher. 1995.

133. Policy Experiences and Issues in the Baltics, Russia, and Other Countries of the Former Soviet Union, edited by Daniel A. Citrin and Ashok K. Lahiri. 1995.

132. Financial Fragilities in Latin America: The 1980s and 1990s, by Liliana Rojas-Suárez and Steven R. Weisbrod. 1995.

131. Capital Account Convertibility: Review of Experience and Implications for IMF Policies, by staff teams headed by Peter J. Quirk and Owen Evans. 1995.

130. Challenges to the Swedish Welfare State, by Desmond Lachman, Adam Bennett, John H. Green, Robert Hagemann, and Ramana Ramaswamy. 1995.

129. IMF Conditionality: Experience Under Stand-By and Extended Arrangements. Part II: Background Papers. Susan Schadler, Editor, with Adam Bennett, Maria Carkovic, Louis Dicks-Mireaux, Mauro Mecagni, James H.J. Morsink, and Miguel A. Savastano. 1995.

128. IMF Conditionality: Experience Under Stand-By and Extended Arrangements. Part I: Key Issues and Findings, by Susan Schadler, Adam Bennett, Maria Carkovic, Louis Dicks-Mireaux, Mauro Mecagni, James H.J. Morsink, and Miguel A. Savastano. 1995.

127. Road Maps of the Transition: The Baltics, the Czech Republic, Hungary, and Russia, by Biswajit Banerjee, Vincent Koen, Thomas Krueger, Mark S. Lutz, Michael Marrese, and Tapio O. Saavalainen. 1995.

126. The Adoption of Indirect Instruments of Monetary Policy, by a Staff Team headed by William E. Alexander, Tomás J.T. Baliño, and Charles Enoch. 1995.

125. United Germany: The First Five Years—Performance and Policy Issues, by Robert Corker, Robert A. Feldman, Karl Habermeier, Hari Vittas, and Tessa van der Willigen. 1995.

124. Saving Behavior and the Asset Price "Bubble" in Japan: Analytical Studies, edited by Ulrich Baumgartner and Guy Meredith. 1995.

123. Comprehensive Tax Reform: The Colombian Experience, edited by Parthasarathi Shome. 1995.

122. Capital Flows in the APEC Region, edited by Mohsin S. Khan and Carmen M. Reinhart. 1995.

121. Uganda: Adjustment with Growth, 1987–94, by Robert L. Sharer, Hema R. De Zoysa, and Calvin A. McDonald. 1995.

120. Economic Dislocation and Recovery in Lebanon, by Sena Eken, Paul Cashin, S. Nuri Erbas, Jose Martelino, and Adnan Mazarei. 1995.

119. Singapore: A Case Study in Rapid Development, edited by Kenneth Bercuson with a staff team comprising Robert G. Carling, Aasim M. Husain, Thomas Rumbaugh, and Rachel van Elkan. 1995.

118. Sub-Saharan Africa: Growth, Savings, and Investment, by Michael T. Hadjimichael, Dhaneshwar Ghura, Martin Mühleisen, Roger Nord, and E. Murat Uçer. 1995.

117. Resilience and Growth Through Sustained Adjustment: The Moroccan Experience, by Saleh M. Nsouli, Sena Eken, Klaus Enders, Van-Can Thai, Jörg Decressin, and Filippo Cartiglia, with Janet Bungay. 1995.

116. Improving the International Monetary System: Constraints and Possibilities, by Michael Mussa, Morris Goldstein, Peter B. Clark, Donald J. Mathieson, and Tamim Bayoumi. 1994.

115. Exchange Rates and Economic Fundamentals: A Framework for Analysis, by Peter B. Clark, Leonardo Bartolini, Tamim Bayoumi, and Steven Symansky. 1994.

114. Economic Reform in China: A New Phase, by Wanda Tseng, Hoe Ee Khor, Kalpana Kochhar, Dubravko Mihaljek, and David Burton. 1994.

113. Poland: The Path to a Market Economy, by Liam P. Ebrill, Ajai Chopra, Charalambos Christofides, Paul Mylonas, Inci Otker, and Gerd Schwartz. 1994.

112. The Behavior of Non-Oil Commodity Prices, by Eduardo Borensztein, Mohsin S. Khan, Carmen M. Reinhart, and Peter Wickham. 1994.

111. The Russian Federation in Transition: External Developments, by Benedicte Vibe Christensen. 1994.

110. Limiting Central Bank Credit to the Government: Theory and Practice, by Carlo Cottarelli. 1993.

109. The Path to Convertibility and Growth: The Tunisian Experience, by Saleh M. Nsouli, Sena Eken, Paul Duran, Gerwin Bell, and Zühtü Yücelik. 1993.

108. Recent Experiences with Surges in Capital Inflows, by Susan Schadler, Maria Carkovic, Adam Bennett, and Robert Kahn. 1993.

107. China at the Threshold of a Market Economy, by Michael W. Bell, Hoe Ee Khor, and Kalpana Kochhar with Jun Ma, Simon N'guiamba, and Rajiv Lall. 1993.

106. Economic Adjustment in Low-Income Countries: Experience Under the Enhanced Structural Adjustment Facility, by Susan Schadler, Franek Rozwadowski, Siddharth Tiwari, and David O. Robinson. 1993.

105. The Structure and Operation of the World Gold Market, by Gary O'Callaghan. 1993.

104. Price Liberalization in Russia: Behavior of Prices, Household Incomes, and Consumption During the First Year, by Vincent Koen and Steven Phillips. 1993.

103. Liberalization of the Capital Account: Experiences and Issues, by Donald J. Mathieson and Liliana Rojas-Suárez. 1993.

102. Financial Sector Reforms and Exchange Arrangements in Eastern Europe. Part I: Financial Markets and Intermediation, by Guillermo A. Calvo and Manmohan S. Kumar. Part II: Exchange Arrangements of Previously Centrally Planned Economies, by Eduardo Borensztein and Paul R. Masson. 1993.

101. Spain: Converging with the European Community, by Michel Galy, Gonzalo Pastor, and Thierry Pujol. 1993.

100. The Gambia: Economic Adjustment in a Small Open Economy, by Michael T. Hadjimichael, Thomas Rumbaugh, and Eric Verreydt. 1992.

99. Mexico: The Strategy to Achieve Sustained Economic Growth, edited by Claudio Loser and Eliot Kalter. 1992.

98. Albania: From Isolation Toward Reform, by Mario I. Blejer, Mauro Mecagni, Ratna Sahay, Richard Hides, Barry Johnston, Piroska Nagy, and Roy Pepper. 1992.

97. Rules and Discretion in International Economic Policy, by Manuel Guitián. 1992.

96. Policy Issues in the Evolving International Monetary System, by Morris Goldstein, Peter Isard, Paul R. Masson, and Mark P. Taylor. 1992.

Note: For information on the title and availability of Occasional Papers not listed, please consult the IMF Publications Catalog or contact IMF Publication Services.